AUSTRALIAN WAR HEROES

THEY SHALL NOT GROW OLD

Published by Brolga Publishing Pty Ltd
ABN 46 063 962 443
PO Box 12544, A'Beckett St, VIC, 8006, Australia
email: markzocchi@brolgapublishing.com.au

National Library of Australia Cataloguing-in-Publication entry

> Author: Ferguson, Ian, 1941-
> Title: Aussie war heroes : they shall not grow old / Ian Ferguson.
> ISBN: 9781922036520 (pbk.)
> Notes: Includes bibliographical references and index.
> Subjects: Heroes--Australia--Biography
>   War--Causes.
>   War.
>   Victoria Cross--Biography.
>   Australia--Military history, Modern.
> Dewey Number: 920.094

Printed in Indonesia
Cover by David Khan
Design & typeset by Wanissa Somsuphangsri

AUSTRALIAN WAR HEROES

THEY SHALL NOT GROW OLD

"They shall grow not old, as we that are left grow old:
Age shall not weary them, nor the years condemn.
At the going down of the sun, and in the morning,
We will remember them."

("For the Fallen", Laurence Binyon)

DEDICATION

This book is respectfully dedicated to the many brave Australian men and women, who have not returned from wars in which our nation became engaged.

ACKNOWLEDGEMENTS

Thanks once more to my wife, Ann, for her valued support and proof reading skills.

I am also extremely grateful to my lawn bowling club colleague, Les Wight, for lending me many valuable research books from his extensive war history collection.

First hand information about the Vietnam War, provided by John Thompson and Robin Leahy, is also much appreciated, and adds greatly to the authenticity of the book's contents. Many thanks also Robin, for supplying those excellent Vietnam War photographs. I am also indebted to Ian and Marjorie Wisken, for allowing me to use their extensive collection of Western Front war cemetery photographs.

Ian Ferguson, May 2012

CONTENTS

CHAPTER ONE:

PRE-ANZAC ENCOUNTERS

Many people believe that Australians were first blooded in war on 25th April 1915, after landing at Gallipoli with their New Zealand comrades. This belief is incorrect. Volunteers from "the land down under" participated in three other international combats, well before their legendary World War 1 encounters with the Turks.

Residents in the then youngest colony of the British Empire, frequently referred to themselves as being "Australian Britons". Consequently, the death of General Gordon in a minor Sudan conflict in 1885, motivated hundreds of Australian volunteers to embark on a long and arduous North African pilgrimage, to fight alongside their "British brothers".

This strong commitment proved to be an anti-climax. By the time they finally arrived the "paltry affair" was virtually over, and only three Australians received wounds in the minor skirmishes.

Imperialism was still an unofficial religion among Anglo-Saxon Australians in 1899, when the Boer War broke out in

South Africa. "This war will be a grand picnic", predicted one rash observer, when thousands of Sydneysiders cheered off a shipload of excited volunteers.

The storm clouds that hung over Sydney that day proved to be an ominous omen. In the veldt, complacent British generals underestimated the skill and commitment of the South Africans, who were fighting for their independence in a familiar terrain. Soon three major towns were under siege, as the determined enemies of Dutch origin, unexpectedly gained the upper hand.

Australian Boer war soldiers

Australian Boer war nurses

In early Boer War conflicts, mixed opinions were voiced about the prowess of the often laconic newcomers from the Antipodes. Some British officers spoke dismissively about the Australians under their command, and maintained they were "poor soldiers". The Boers, however, expressed a growing respect for the newcomers from the south. "The Australians are far more committed than any British troops," was a comment attributed to a Boer combatant, following a crucial battle at Eland River.

The Victoria Cross

The now legendary Australian poet, Andrew Barton "Banjo" Paterson, was full of imperialistic enthusiasm, when he began his war correspondent duties in South Africa. However Paterson soon became disillusioned with the growing casualty rate among the Australians, with 606 paying the ultimate sacrifice from war wounds or disease, before the three-year war ended.

Andrew Barton
Paterson

Australia's first war fatality occurred early in the conflict, when 27 year old Trooper Victor Jones, from Rockhampton Queensland, was killed in action (KIA) in a fierce encounter at Sunnyside Farm.

Overall, Paterson and other Australian observers felt there was little British official recognition of Australian initiative and bravery, even though six Australians were awarded Victoria Crosses (VCs) in South Africa.

The VC award originates from the mid

3

Trooper Victor
Jones

nineteenth century, after a cross bearing Queen Victoria's name was instituted in 1856. The original cross honoured individual acts of bravery from the Crimean War. It was allegedly crafted from bronze, which was collected from a captured cannon.

It remains the most prestigious military award for bravery. All ranks of service are eligible for a VC award, as are civilians serving under military command. The main criteria in the selection process, is to display valour in the presence of the enemy. The VC is regarded as being almost priceless in value.

The current world record for a VC purchase is $A1,214,500. This gargantuan amount was paid by Aussie media tycoon, Kerry Stokes, for the VC awarded in 1915 to Lone Pine hero, Captain Alfred Shout. Stokes subsequently donated Shout's prestigious medal to the Australian War Museum.

Recently, on July 28th 2011, the VC issued to World War11 legend Ted Kenna, was sold to an anonymous buyer for the princely sum of $A1,200,000. This VC recipient's son, Rob Kenna, informed fellow Australians, that it was his late father's wish for the medal to be sold two years after his death, and for the proceeds to be distributed among the Kenna family.

"It was dad's legacy to us," explained an emotional Bob Kenna, "It's not hard to

see it go. **The medal is about Australia, and what the Diggers have done for us. It is a fantastic result for the family…"**

Captain Neville Reginald Howse became our first VC winner. The other Boer War VC recipients from Australia, were Trooper J.H. Bisdee and Lieutenant G.G. Wylly, (both from Tasmania), Western Australian Lieutenant F.W. Bell, Sergeant J. Rogers from NSW, and Lieutenant L.C. Maygar from Victoria.

Captain Neville
Howse

> **"Did you think I would leave you dying,**
> **When there's room on my horse for two?**
> **Climb up here, we'll soon be flying,**
> **I can go just as fast with two.**
> **Can you feel Joe, I'm all a tremble?**
> **Perhaps it's the battle's noise.**
> **But I think it's that I remember**
> **When we were two little boys."**

Trooper J.H.
Bisdee

"Two Little Boys" was composed by Morse and Madden in 1902, when the Boer War was coming to a close. Decades later its popularity was rejuvenated, after Rolf Harris, the talented Australian artist and entertainer, re-introduced it to global audiences.

The stanza quoted above, relates closely to war action of that time, when horses were highly valued in combat situations.

Neville Howse volunteered for active

5

service in South Africa, and became a member of the NSW Medical Corps. The then Taree doctor was awarded a VC after he rescued a fallen trumpeter. Heavy gunfire killed Howse's horse during the rescue. Consequently, he carried his wounded comrade to safety, after providing medical treatment.

When the Boer War ended, Neville Howse became a prominent public figure in Australia. He was twice mayor of the City of Orange, and in 1922 he won the Federal seat of Calare for the National Party. During his seven years of parliamentary life, Neville House held several ministerial portfolios. The Howse family continued to remain prominent in Australian politics, as between 1946 and 1960, Neville's son, John Howse, became the sitting member for Calare.

Neville Howse returned to military service with the advent of World War 1. He rose to the rank of Lieutenant Colonel when he was appointed as a principal medical officer, and he later assisted wounded soldiers to evacuate during the early days of the Gallipoli campaign. The formidable doctor became highly critical about the standard of medical care, which was then available in the Dardanelles.

Around that time, Neville Howse married, and he later became the father of five children. In 1930 his search for a cancer cure took him to London, but it was there that Major-General Sir Neville Howse (VC, KCB, KCMG, K.St.J) died at the age of 66.

Trooper John Hutton Bisdee was participating in an advance scouting party that was ambushed by a group of Boers. He, and five others, was badly wounded in the attack. However Bisdee managed to place an injured Major Brooks on his own horse, and transported him to safety under heavy fire. Later Bisdee received a VC - the first to be awarded in an Australian unit.

John Bisdee survived the South African campaign, and when World War 1 began, he enlisted in the AIF as a Captain in the 12th Light Horse Brigade. His wife accompanied him to conflicts in the Middle East, where she became highly valued for her work in AIF canteens.

Lieutenant GuyWylly

Bisdee VC reached the rank of Major, before his discharge from the army in 1920. In civilian life, John Bisdee continued to farm his Tasmanian property, until he died at the age of 61.

Lieutenant Guy George Egerton Wylly was involved in the same Boer War action as Bidsee, and, despite personally suffering serious wounds, he saved Corporal Brown's life. Wylly provided his injured comrade with a horse and ground cover, until safety was reached.

Guy Wylly was born to be a soldier, His father, Edward, was an officer in the Indian army, and following Guy's birth in Tasmania, the future VC winner spent much of his childhood years in India.

In 1918 Wylly was awarded a DSO for his distinguished service in the Middle East during World War 1. He reached the rank of Major, before retiring from the army in 1933. Guy Wylly then worked for the Retired

Lieutenant
Frederick Bell

Private James
Rogers

Officers Employment Bureau. Wylly VC later died at the age of 81 in Surrey.

Lieutenant Frederick William Bell from Perth was with his unit, when they survived fierce bombardments from the Boers. However Bell returned to the action, to recover a comrade who had fallen from his horse. He placed the injured man on his own steed, and provided cover for him until safety was reached.

Fred Bell was an adventurous man, who lived an eventful life. Before volunteering for action in the Boer War, he worked as a cashier with the Western Australian Customs Department. Then, once hostilities ceased on the veldt, Fred Bell remained in Africa for much of his young adult years.

At first he was an Assistant District Officer in British Somaliland, where he was seriously injured after being savagely mauled by a lion. The advent of World War 1 saw Fred Bell again volunteer for military service, and in this conflict he was promoted to the rank of Captain.

When the Great War terminated, Fred Bell became a District Commissioner in Kenya. At the age of 47 he married a divorcee, and 22 years after she died, he remarried a widow. This VC recipient returned briefly to WA, but Fred Bell was residing in England, when he died at the age of 79.

Private James Rogers from Moama in NSW

rescued a grounded Lieutenant by placing him on his own horse. It carried the fortunate soldier 800 metres through heavy fire until safe refuge was reached. Rogers then returned to rescue another two men, and transported them to safety, after retrieving riderless horses.

At that time, James Rogers was serving as a Sergeant with the South African Constabulary of the South African Forces. When World War 1 began, Rogers was elevated to the rank of Lieutenant in the AIF. However James Rogers was so badly wounded at Anzac Cove, that he was repatriated to Australia, after being declared medically unfit for further combat.

James Rogers recovered well from his war injuries, and he was aged 86 when he died in Sydney. The Moama VC recipient was finally buried at the Springvale Crematorium in Melbourne.

In another fierce Boer War encounter, soggy ground forced Lieutenant Leslie Cecil Maygar to dismount from his steed, when he was transporting a wounded comrade to safety. The injured man stayed on the horse until safety was reached, while Maygar made his way back on foot.

Maygar was a grazier at Euroa in Victoria's north-east, before volunteering for war action in South Africa. The beginning of his military career on the veldt certainly proved to be an anti-climax, as L.C. ("Elsie") Maygar was rejected by authorities, because of tooth decay! After overcoming that minor obstacle Maygar served with distinction in both the Boer War, and at Gallipoli in 1915. There he was promoted to the position of Major, and the revered commander of the 3rd Light Horse Regiment was probably one of the last Anzacs to depart from the Dardanelles, when the allies withdrew their forces.

"Breaker" Morant

Leslie Maygar, (VC, DSO, VD), became revered for his fine horsemanship and strong leadership qualities. During his tour of duty in Sinai and Palestine, Leslie Maygar was awarded a DSO. He later lost his life in World War 1 action in North Africa, while commanding the legendary 8th Light Horse Regiment. Predictably, Maygar was killed while leading "the last great cavalry charge in history", at Beersheba on 1st November, 1917.

Justice may decree that these first six VC winners deserve to be remembered as being Australia's true heroes from the Boer War. However, accolades are not always accorded to the most deserving. Consequently, it is the controversial Harry "Breaker" Morant, who remains our most memorable Boer War participant.

Morant was born in England in 1864, and he was 29 years of age when he emigrated to Townsville. Around that area of north Queensland, Morant became a skilled horse breaker, which gained him the nickname of "Breaker". He was a personable and educated man, and soon gained an infamous reputation due to his dare-devil behaviour and excessive womanising. At one time he was married briefly to Daisy Bates, who later became famous for her welfare work in isolated aboriginal communities.

The outbreak of war in South Africa in 1899, provided Breaker with an opportunity to escape from various debts he had incurred, and the many women he had betrayed. Most volunteers from the Australian colonies believed the Boers would be quickly defeated, and, once this mission was achieved, Morant hoped to return to his native England. By the time training exercises were completed in Adelaide, Morant had become a Lance Corporal, and he departed for South Africa on 26th January 1900.

His horse riding skills on veldt battlefields, resulted in Morant becoming a despatch rider in the conflict for London's "Daily Telegraph". Around that time Breaker became engaged to the sister of his close army friend, Captain Frederick Percy Hunt.

By 1901, both Morant and Hunt had enlisted with a highly regarded unit called the Bushveldt Carabineers, but on August 5th Hunt was brutally killed during a fierce battle waged on a Boer farmhouse. When an enemy wearing Hunt's uniform was captured, the enraged Morant and other Carabineers killed him and other prisoners as well. One of those executed was a civilian; a German priest, who was believed to be actively associated with the enemy.

Following the unlawful executions, Morant and six others were arrested. Breaker's defiant attitude to his British captors won him few friends, before court martial proceedings began.

In the military court, Morant admitted to some killings, but claimed he had previously been ordered to take no prisoners. The trial in Pietersburg was briefly postponed when a Boer attack threatened the town. Morant was one of many who fought bravely to turn back the enemy.

The valour he displayed then did little to help his cause. All three Australians charged were found guilty of murdering the Boer prisoners, but cleared of the charge of killing the German civilian. Both Morant and Peter Handcock were sentenced to death by firing squad. Some believed this harsh sentence was handed down to placate those European governments, who still expressed outrage about the death of the German priest.

It was the renowned British commander, Lord Kitchener, who signed the convicted Australian's execution orders. Later, well after both men were shot dead, Kitchener admitted he had previously ordered the punishment of execution, for any enemy found wearing British uniforms.

Prior to their deaths by firing squad on February 27th 1902, both Morant and Handcock refused to be blindfolded. George Witton, the other Australian found guilty, received life imprisonment, but he was only in custody for 28 months before the British House of Commons overturned his sentence on 11th August, 1905. The two British officers also found guilty of the charges, only received dishonourable discharges as a penalty. George Witton later wrote a book titled "Scapegoats of the Empire", a publication which criticised Kitchener's role in the tragic outcome.

Back in Australia the executions, and certain aspects of the trial, alarmed some sections of the public. Court proceedings had been conducted secretly, which was contrary to regulations. Furthermore, after the trials ended, vital court transcripts could not be found.

Lord Kitchener later travelled to Australia, and part of his good will mission included a visit to Peter Handcock's home town of Bathurst, to unveil a Boer War memorial. The visit of the esteemed British General attracted some controversy. Handcock's widow at one stage threatened to publicly confront Kitchener over her husband's execution. Later, when the memorial was revealed for the first time to a large local audience, Peter Handcock was not included on the list of Bathurst Boer War casualties. It was only after Kitchener departed, that Handcock's name was added to the list of locals who had died for Britain and the Empire, in the South African conflict.

Over a century has passed since the controversial executions were carried out, but Breaker Morant still enjoys a celebrity status of Ned Kelly like proportions. In 1980 Bruce Beresford directed a blockbuster movie titled "Breaker Morant", with Edward Woodward playing the leading role, while Bryan Brown portrayed Handcock.

Supporters of Morant have long defended the popular larrikin's role in South Africa. Finally, in March 2010, an Australian Federal Parliamentary Committee presented a petition which requested Queen Elizabeth 11 to grant a posthumous pardon for Harry "Breaker" Morant.

Former Australian Navy lawyer, Commander James (Jim) Unkles, was the main spokesperson for Morant's support group. Unkles claimed the dual executions were an unjust stain on Australian history, and should be removed. He still contends the legal processes followed were unjust, even by the standards of the day. Furthermore, an official posthumous pardon for all three men would make an enormous difference to surviving relatives, and indeed all Australians.

Unkles' views are not shared by all. Historian Craig Wilcox maintains those killed by Morant's group were not battlefield prisoners but civilians. Consequently the executions were a gross injustice, and should not be condoned.

The Commonwealth Government's petition for Morant's pardon was presented to the British Government, but in November 2010 it was rejected. Dr Liam Fox, the British Secretary of State for Defence, claimed no new primary evidence had been presented to justify overturning the original court-martial decision.

On October 20th 2011, Unkles' efforts to have the case reopened received a boost when the then Federal Attorney-General, Senator Robert McClelland intervened in the matter. McClelland announced that he would write to his British counterpart, stating that Morant, Handcock and Witton were not given a fair trial by the standards of the day.

This new development still falls short of calling for a full pardon, and by early 2012 communications between the Australian and British governments on this issue appeared to have stalled However, Jim Unkles and his supporters are still heartened by the Commonwealth's cautious intervention in this controversial stalemate, which has now been debated for more than a century.

The final pre-Gallipoli war action, popularly known as the Boxer Rebellion, occurred in China between 1900 and 1901, and once more Australian volunteers responded to Britain's imperialistic needs. Like the Sudan skirmish, the Boxer Rebellion was a very low key affair for our soldiers, and the six Australian fatalities which occurred were all caused by illness.

CHAPTER TWO:

GALLIPOLI : A ROMANCE WHICH SOURED

**"They went with songs to the battle, they were young,
Straight of limb, true of eye, steady and aglow…
They were staunch to the end against odds uncounted;
They fell with their faces to the foe."**

"For The Fallen" was written by Laurence Binyon in 1914. The above stanza of his now famous poem, well describes the excited anticipation which gripped many young Aussies, when the prospect of war beckoned.

The vast majority of Australians showed an eager readiness to be involved in a major armed conflict, well before hostilities began in far off Europe. Defending "the mother country" (England), and the British Empire, were ideals passionately embraced across the young nation. Ironically, the vast majority who expressed these grandiose sentiments, had never been to England, and were never likely to travel there in the future.

At that time, many Australians really regarded themselves as being transplanted from the British Isles. Even our second

Alfred Deakin

William Bridges

Prime Minister, Alfred Deakin, once proudly described himself as being "an independent Australian-Briton".

In the first decade of the 20th century, imperialistic fervour grew even stronger, as tensions escalated rapidly between European nations. The flash point for World War 1 conflict occurred in the Balkans city of Sarajevo on 28th June 1914, when Archbishop Franz Ferdinand was assassinated. By the end of July, Austria, Hungary and Russia had all mobilised forces. An aggressive response to the far off crisis was also evident in Australia, well before any major action began.

Major-General William Bridges, a Scottish born Australian, stamped the imperialist badge on our own army from its very inception. In 1911, after Bridges was appointed Commander of the newly formed Duntroon Military College, he named the first armed forces group the Australian Imperial Force (AIF). Bridges felt such a title emphasised the strong links which existed between Australia and the British Empire. His decision was well accepted across the country, but our example was not followed by other Empire nations, such as New Zealand and Canada.

To the general public, the anticipated conflict soon resembled a crusade. Many did indeed go "with songs to the battle", and it was evident that some Australians were prepared to "celebrate" war. Battlefields developed the image of resembling a sports oval, from which Australia would walk away with a cup, after gaining an inevitable victory.

The nation's leaders supported imperialist actions. At a public rally on 31st July 1914, the soon to be elected Prime Minister, Andrew Fisher, gained strong support around the country, following his unequivocal declaration that:

"Australians will stand beside their own, to help defend her to our last man, and our last shilling".

"Her" of course referred to the "mother country" or Britain, and there was complete bi-partisan political support for a strong Australian commitment. The day before war was officially declared, the new Prime Minister, Joseph Cook, offered to place Australian vessels under complete control of the British Admiralty. Cook also predicted that a minimum of 20,000 servicemen would volunteer their services to Britain, wherever they were needed for active involvement.

Predictably, the nation supported their leaders' united stand with much enthusiasm. After Britain declared war on Germany at midnight on 4th August 1914, crowds sang "God Save the King" on the streets, and bands played "Rule Britannia" in cafes and theatres. Next day, at Melbourne University, when lectures concluded, students sang the national anthem, (then applicable to both Australia and England), with much gusto.

The national media was influential in promoting our perceived responsibilities to Britain and the Empire, and, once the war began, battles tended to be glamorised. The flamboyant English war columnist, Ellis Ashmead-Bartlett, was especially popular with his literary flourishes. He and other war front journalists noted "fallen" rather than "dead" soldiers in their columns, and those killed were honoured for "paying the supreme sacrifice". "Defeats" tended to be redefined as "good progress skirmishes", and impressive numbers of "gallant" officers were paid due homage. Overall, it seemed that God was an Anglican to the Anglo-Saxon world of the early 20th century, and the strongest swear word one could expect to read, was written as "d..n".

The Gallipoli campaign occurred nearly one hundred years ago, but the myths surrounding battle sites such as Anzac Cove, are still viewed with much nostalgia by both young and old Australians. Gallipoli, according to Prime Minister Hughes in 1916, was where:

"Australia put on the toga of manhood".

Similar sentiments are still expressed today, when large dawn crowds gather annually on 25th April near war memorials, which honour Australian service men and women. Some, whose names are forever carved in stone, have been dead for nearly 100 years.

Young faces and old are seen on those chilly autumn mornings, in hamlets and cities around the nation. Geoff Page describes the yearly tradition tellingly, in his poem titled "Small Town Memorials".

No matter how small, every town has one;
Maybe just the obelisk,
A few names inlaid;
More often full scale granite...
Sometimes not even a town,
A clearing of houses,...

**Glimpsed on a back road
Will have one**.

Past local communities have worked hard to fittingly honour the men and women who served in various wars. In 1920, in the small NSW south coastal town of Thirroul, the local's war memorial was finally completed. Service groups conducted raffles and ran produce stalls to raise the nine hundred pounds needed to finance the project. It was especially noted, that Thirroul school children donated just under a shilling towards this worthy cause.

On a grander scale, in November 1941, the National War Museum was officially opened. This prestigious structure is one of the most expensive projects ever undertaken in Australia. The thousands of visitors who regularly flock to see its exhibits, archives and libraries each year, do so free of charge.

Today, the legends associated with wartime service seem even more compelling, for those increasing number of Aussies who make the "pilgrimage" to the Dardanelles. In his fine book, "Gallipoli", Les Carlyon muses that **Gallipoli is a place of the mind: everyone who goes there sees it the way they want.**

Battle sites in that area of Turkey certainly still seem to evoke an intensely personal response among many visitors. Most Australian households in 1915 had direct or indirect links to World War 1 casualties, and to some, the tragedies of the conflict never ended. Today the graveyard tributes found in this now pristine area of Turkey, still express both grief and imperialistic pride. Such conflicting emotions are inextricably linked to Australian memories of the first Anzacs.

"A Place Is Vacant in Our Home Which Can Never Be Filled", is one anguished tribute.

Those tragic words were carved on the headstone of Private H. Andrews, who was serving in the Army Service Corps, when he was KIA on 19th November, 1915. Andrews was 46 when he died, and he is one of hundreds buried at Gallipoli.

"Rest Dear Son, Rest, Sadly Missed" is another heartrending epitaph, written as a tribute to Trooper R.E. Cummings of the 10th Australian Light Horse Brigade. He was KIA on 7th September, 1915.

"Only a Boy, But Died as a Man for Liberty and Freedom", was a Mum and Dad tribute to the late Private H.J. Burton. He was 18, and serving in the 23rd BN Australian Infantry, when he died in action on 30th November, 1915.

War Grave shots from Gallipoli

Imperialistic messages are prominent in many Gallipoli tributes. Tourists are informed that 28 year old Private Peter A. Smith, of the 25th BN Australian Infantry Corps, **"Gave Up His life For His King and Country",** and 25 year old Bombardier W.H. Benson, of the Australian Field Artillery, paid **"The Supreme Sacrifice for God, His King and**

Country" on 21st November, 1915.

Various cemeteries around Gallipoli contain similar tributes. The burial site at Lone Pine became the final resting place for nearly 1,000 Anzacs, and many unknown soldiers are included among the dead.

Crowd sizes at the annual Anzac Cove service in the Dardanelles now exceed 30,000. Authorities are considering placing quotas in order to restrict the growing number of visitors.

Infrastructures around landmark battle fields are currently struggling to cope. By June 2010 Turkish authorities were considering the construction of a sea wall, in order to control erosion problems around Gallipoli. Unfortunately, the thousands of people, who pour into the area every April, are threatening the very area they come to revere.

Some believe that the myths associated with Anzac Cove, Lone Pine, The Nek and other almost sacred sites, tend to be exaggerated. After all, fewer lives were lost in this eight month conflict than on the two Western Front battlefields of Fromelles and Pozieres. Perhaps this growing public involvement with Gallipoli memorial services, unintentionally denigrates brave and successful achievements in other important war engagements.

One telling example occurred at Beersheba on November 1st 1917. In this North African conflict, the Australian 8th Light Horse Brigade achieved a memorable victory, with "the last great cavalry charge in history". However one does not hear about memorial candles being lit at that battle site, and scores of pilgrims don't flock to anniversary services in Beersheba.

Furthermore, the Gallipoli campaign, unlike the fall of

Paul Keating

Singapore, never directly threatened Australia. However that 1942 disaster, which occurred much closer to our shores, seems almost insignificant in comparison. Perhaps the same anomaly applies to the real importance of our World War 11 victory against invading Japanese forces, on New Guinea's Kokoda Trail. Former Prime Minister Paul Keating certainly believes that turning back the Japanese forces remains an underrated achievement. In a 1992 address near that historic battle site, in the re-named country of Papua-New Guinea, Keating stated that **"This was the place where the depth and soul of the Australian nation was confirmed...Gallipoli was a defeat, (but) Kokoda was a victory."**

Between August and September 1914, an excited anticipation grew in communities across the country, as the Australian Government busily began war preparations. By the end of October, 26 Australian and New Zealand warships were docked in the deep waters of King George Sound off Western Australia. On 1st November, the first of our World War 1 volunteers began their long voyage to the Middle East. On route, off the Cocos Islands, members of the fleet sank the German Raider vessel "Emden". This early success greatly raised the morale of the first diggers.

Some historians believe that the term

"digger" originated from the gold rush days of early Australia, when a spirit of camaraderie quickly developed among the early prospectors or diggers. Many were from diverse foreign backgrounds, but they became strongly united when their democratic rights were ignored by heavy handed government authorities on the Ballarat diggings. Simmering resentment between the two groups culminated in the battle of the Eureka Stockade, at Bakery Hill on 3rd December 1854. Miners in Australia finally gained the right to vote from this momentous event. Consequently, the Eureka Stockade, which has since been labelled "the cradle of Australian democracy", became a significant victory for the diggers who defied government authorities on that now historic site.

Scene of Anzac Cove

The Australian and New Zealand Army Corps (Anzacs) first began gruelling army training in Egypt, under the leadership of the British officer, Brigadier-General Sir William Birdwood. The small, energetic Birdwood was one of the better British officers to command World War1 diggers. He went on to become an inspirational leader to many, and he was respected by soldiers for his common sense approach to problems.

The first diggers from the Antipodes certainly presented problems in Egypt. Most of the 20-34 year old predominantly bachelor servicemen, resented the parade ground type discipline favoured by the majority of British officers. The Australians soon developed a reputation for being disrespectful and loutish soldiers, who enjoyed whoring and brawling around the seamier areas of Cairo.

Thankfully a looming battle assignment interrupted their unruly behaviour, but their training camps in the desert unfortunately had little relevance for the formidable mission which lay ahead. In Egypt they had no hands-on experience with grenades, periscopes, howitzers or machine guns, weapons which their future enemy in Turkey utilised very effectively.

By December the British General Staff in London formulated a plan which author Peter Cochrane later described as "a gambler's dream". The potential rewards from the ambitious strategy were indeed enticing- securing the Suez Canal, and opening up an essential supply link to Russia via the Black Sea. This, the British war-chiefs believed, would be achieved by forcing a sea and land passage through the Dardanelles. Then the Turkish capital of Constantinople, (now Istanbul), would be virtually obliterated by fierce bombing attacks.

In his book "Australians at War", Cochrane described the overall Dardanelles strategy as one that "aimed for maximum results with minimum investment". Never-the-less, it was the

Anzac forces in Egypt who were assigned this "mission impossible". They sailed from Alexandria to the Dardanelles, on the 4th April, 1915.

At the outset, the hastily formed plan began to unravel. The diggers believed they would land on an open plain, and little resistance to the invasion was expected from the Turkish defenders. In actuality the 3rd Brigade landed about a kilometre from the intended safer starting point. The first invaders became easy targets for the skilled enemy marksmen, when they mounted a brave bayonet charge up the steep cliffs. Over 600 men died at Anzac Cove in that first landing.

**"How well I remember that terrible day,
When the blood stained the sand and the water.
And how in that hell that we called Suvla Bay,
We were butchered like lambs at the slaughter."**

(Extract from "And the Band Played Waltzing Matilda", written by Scottish-born Australian songwriter, Eric Bogle, in 1971.)

Butchered indeed. The allied invasion at Suvla Bay actually occurred some months later, and signalled the start of the August offensive. However the carnage among allied forces at both landing points was immense.

After the ill-fated landing failed dismally at Anzac Cove, the terrible slaughter grew even worse. In fact, over 2,000 Anzacs were either killed or wounded, during the first few fateful days. However within a month, the beachhead was made relatively secure by the invading forces, and a stalemate developed between the Turkish and Anzac soldiers in their

Eric Bogle

respective trenches.

Both the first landing and the campaign in general, tended to be glamorised by media outlets back in Australia. However the harsh reality of life in the trenches was anything but enticing. Overall the days were uncomfortable and monotonous at best, but the constant artillery fire, along with lice and the threat of disease, mostly produced a highly dangerous environment.

"**The worst things here, (Turks excepted), are the flies in millions, the lice…everlasting bully beef and biscuits, and too little water.**" (A description attributed to Captain D.G Campbell, who was later KIA on 6th August 1915).

Medical aid for the many wounded Anzacs was woefully inadequate. In the hospital ships anchored off-shore, it was estimated that only one nurse and two medical aides were available to care for up to 250 patients.

Some believe that Australia came of age on the world stage in the Gallipoli campaign, but, if so the maturity came at a dreadful cost. The Nek campaign, which began on 7th August 1915, was the most shambolic and disastrous of all Gallipoli engagements. Planned support and cover fire failed to eventuate, communication between command centre and the front line broke down, and artillery support for the engagement mistakenly ended seven minutes before the cavalry like charges began.

This unexpected halt to the artillery attack, allowed the Turks to safely regroup. Consequently the Australian 8th and 10th Light Horse Brigades were slaughtered by the enemy marksmen, when they attempted to seize the narrow Nek position with their futile bayonet charges.

Estimates claim that the first line of Anzacs was slain within seconds, after advancing only a few metres. The same mindless slaughter occurred with the second line of Horsemen, which activated some battalion commanders to question the strategy. However Lieutenant-Colonel Antill, from the safety of command centre, repeatedly ordered the 3rd and 4th line of soldiers to "push on". By then many realised that death was the only outcome.

"Goodbye cobber, God bless you," stated Trooper Harold Rush to a comrade, before he advanced into a fatal hail of bullets.

The catastrophic outcome from the Nek disaster was that only 47 of the original 550 soldiers survived, in their futile attempts to secure a worthless area of land which was little bigger than a tennis court. No strategic benefits were obvious, and historian Geoffrey Blainey summed up the tragic debacle with these words

"...the loss of all those talented people who would have become Prime Ministers, and Premiers, judges, divines, engineers, teachers, doctors, poets, inventors, farmers, the mayors of towns and leaders of trade unions, and fathers of another generation of Australians".

Incompetent leadership was clearly a major factor in the

Alymer Hunter-Weston

Mustafa Kemal Ataturk

huge casualty rate at Gallipoli. Belatedly, by October 1915, after the Nek battlefield debacle was evaluated, the charming but indecisive General Sir Ian Standish Monteith Hamilton, (then commander of the Allies Mediterranean Expeditionary Force), was recalled to London. However other dangerously incompetent officers were retained, and in some cases even promoted, despite their legacy of ongoing failures.

It appeared common, for military leaders of that era, to display a callous attitude towards the welfare of troops under their command. Mustafa Kemal Ataturk, the still revered World War 1 Turkish leader, once famously informed his soldiers that

"I am not ordering you to attack. I am ordering you to die".

A similar disregard for human life was evident in the World War 1 allied leadership group.

"Casualties? What do I care for casualties?" was the alleged reaction of General Sir Alymer Hunter-Weston, after receiving information about the growing death toll, during the early months of the Gallipoli campaign. The same insensitive officer, also spoke with relish about "blooding the pups", before young men became engaged in trench warfare. Hunter-Weston was then the Commander of the 29th Division, and it comes as no surprise to hear, that the luckless Anzacs under his command, dubbed him "the butcher of Helles".

Later in the Gallipoli campaign, Hunter-Weston was inexplicably elevated to the rank of Corps Commander, a decision that failed to impress many, including Australian author, Les Carlyon.

In his excellent book, "Gallipoli", Carlyon is scathing about Hunter-Weston's leadership skills, and he also criticises the performances of other British officers in the Dardanelles campaign, such as Sir Alexander Godley and Sir Frederick Stoppford. The common strategy for such officers was to oversee bayonet charges against heavily fortified Turkish trenches in broad daylight. Furthermore, when such tactics failed, the same blueprint for action was invariably repeated next day!

Carlyon's most trenchant comments, however, are directed at the performances of Lieutenant-Colonel John "Bull" Antill, an Australian officer, who largely oversaw the mass slaughter which occurred at the Nek in August 1915.

It was Antill who ignored pleas from divisional commanders to end the suicidal Anzac bayonet charges towards the well fortified Turkish trenches. Seemingly those fine young men from the 8th and 10th Light Horse Regiments were no more than "cannon fodder" to "Bull" Antill. His antiquated tactics would probably not have succeeded against weapons used decades before, in the American Civil War.

Over 500 young men lost their lives within minutes at the Nek; a tragic outcome which proved that incompetent leadership, and the difficult terrain, represented bigger problems to the Anzacs than their Turkish opponents.

Antill later failed to impress observers at Sinai in the Western

Desert campaign. However, after ill health forced his repatriation to Australia, he was made a Companion of the Order of St, Michael and St. George. Inexplicably, honours continued to flow his way, for when "Bull" Antill resigned from army service in 1924, he was named an honorary Major-General.

In total, approximately 50,000 Australian servicemen served in Gallipoli. Of those, 8,709 were KIA, while 1,944 received war injuries. The battle of Lone Pine, which the Allies gained within three days during the August offensive, was arguably our major Gallipoli triumph. However the death toll of 2,000 Australians was a huge price to pay for 100 metres of largely meaningless territory. During the gruelling months of the entire campaign, a grudging respect developed for brave Australian soldiers, and seven VCs were awarded to our servicemen at Lone Pine.

Lone Pine

CHAPTER THREE:

OUR FIRST ANZAC VC HEROES

The first and most famous Anzac VC winner was Captain Albert ("Bert") Jacka, whose fearless bravery made him a legendary figure among all future Aussie war heroes, and the general public.

Albert was one of seven children born to Elizabeth and Nathaniel Jacka, when they managed a dairy farm near the Victorian town of Winchelsea. The family soon moved across the state to Wedderburn, where Nathaniel Jacka became a haulage contractor. The relationship between Bert and his moody father was often volatile. Once the issue of conscription became much debated within the family home, the domestic situation became even more strained.

Nathaniel Jacka was a passionate socialist, who deplored the notion of compulsory military service for a "British imperialist war". His more pragmatic son, after battling against numerically superior enemy forces at Gallipoli and the Western Front, believed conscription was an essential policy in the Allied forces' quest for victory. When the much decorated Bert Jacka was afforded a hero's welcome after returning to Melbourne, his father did not attend the public celebrations.

By then Albert Jacka was a strongly built young man of average height. During his developmental years, boxing was one of his passions, but overall there was little evidence from the youthful Bert Jacka's lifestyle, to indicate that he would become a fearless fighting machine.

Jacka's reckless bravery was evident within a month of the Anzacs first landing at Gallipoli. On the 19th May 1915, he was one of a group of four who unsuccessfully attempted a frontal assault on a Turkish trench. Jacka reacted to this setback by crawling over "no man's land" behind the enemy, and launching a brutal surprise attack. The ferocious Australian killed two of the foe with his knife, and shot dead another five. Shortly after the gunfire subsided, Lieutenant Crabbe, his commanding officer, discovered Jacka in the enemy trench, surrounded by corpses, and with an unlit cigarette dangling from his lips.

"Well, I managed to get the beggars, sir", was Bert's greeting comment.

Later this act of heroism by Jacka at Gallipoli was repeated in other Great War battles. In 1916, amid the terrible carnage of Pozieres near the Somme on the Western Front, Bert Jacka's courage and presence of mind virtually saved the day for allied forces, after their line of resistance was briefly broken by the Germans.

During that conflict, when around 40 Aussie Prisoners of War, (POWs), were being led away, Jacka was one of eight soldiers who launched a savage counter attack. Despite being knocked down and wounded in the head and shoulders by bomb blasts, he killed approximately 20 enemy soldiers. This daring intervention released his captured comrades, and his actions were later described as being "the most dramatic act of individual audacity in the history of the A.I.F."

C.E.W. Bean, the renowned war columnist, believed that the two Military Medals, which Jacka gained from Western Front battles, should have been elevated in status, by adding two bars to his existing VC award. Despite his incredible bravery, however, Albert Jacka was never promoted beyond the rank of Captain. Perhaps his tendency to be outspoken, failed to impress some military officers.

The chains of command may have had reservations about the prickly Victorian, but to the soldiers in the 14th Battalion, Bert Jacka became a living legend. One of his comrades eulogised his memory with the following tribute.

"Not we only, but…the whole A.I.F. came to look upon him as a rock of strength that never failed. We of the 14th Battalion never ceased to be thrilled when we …heard ourselves referred to as, "some of Jacka's mob".

Jacka was gifted five hundred pounds and a gold medal by the controversial Melbourne businessman John Wren, after war wounds forced the shy hero to return to Australia. In civilian life Albert Jacka opened an electrical goods and exporting business in Melbourne's CBD. He was soon elected to his local council, and later served as Mayor of St. Kilda. During his years of public life, Bert Jacka became highly regarded for the assistance he gave less fortunate members of the community.

Jacka married his work secretary, Frances Veronica "Vera"

Captain
Albert Jacka

Leonard Keysor

Carey in 1921, and the couple later raised an adopted daughter named Elizabeth, whom they usually called Betty. The seven severe war wounds he suffered, however, along with his exposure to gas warfare on the Western Front, eroded Albert Jacka's health. In 1932 he died prematurely at the age of 39.

Eight fellow Australian VC winners were pall bearers at Albert Jacka's funeral, while past members of his brigade and numerous unemployed people marched behind his hearse. Despite the stifling hot conditions which prevailed on January 19th 1932, at least 6,000 members of the general public witnessed their hero's journey to the St Kilda Cemetery. Today the following epitaph is scribed on his tombstone.

> **"Captain Albert Jacka**
> **VC, MC and Bar. 14th Battalion, A.I.F.**
> **The first VC in the Great War 1914-1918.**
> **A gallant soldier.**
> **An honoured citizen".**

Multiple VCs were awarded at the battle of Lone Pine, which was one of the few Gallipoli victories gained by the first Anzacs. It was the heroic actions of Lance Corporal Leonard Keysor, from the 1st Battalion, which resulted in him becoming one of the recipients.

For almost 50 hours, Keysor risked his own life by throwing back Turkish bombs, so that his unit's forward trenches would be protected. Some of the missiles were well caught by Keysor before they landed, and he then lobbed them back at the enemy. Leonard Keysor was wounded twice during his epic stand, but he survived both Lone Pine and battles on the Western Front.

The English born Keysor had spent ten years in Canada, before briefly working as a clerk in Sydney prior to the start of World War 1. Following his war experiences, Leonard Keysor became an uncompromising advocate for conscription. Keysor was essentially a shy man who shunned publicity. Consequently, it surprised many when he re-enacted his bomb throwing exploits, for the 1927 film titled "For Valour".

After the war ended, Leonard Keysor returned to London, where he married and became a successful businessman. The 65 year old Leonard Keysor was survived by his wife and daughter, when cancer claimed his life in 1951.

Another VC winner was Lieutenant William Symons of the 7th Battalion, who was formerly a Kyneton ironmonger in central Victoria. Symons stoically continued to advance the men under his command, even though the group suffered severe casualties from heavy bombardments. Lieutenant Symons was later badly gassed at Messines on the Western Front, but he recovered his health. At war's end, he had been elevated to the rank of Lieutenant-Colonel. Symons later served in Britain's Home Guard between 1941 and 1944, and he was 58 years of age when he died.

Private John Hamilton from the Third Battalion received his VC after spending six gruelling hours in "no man's land".

Lieutenant
William Symons

Private John
Hamilton

From that dangerous position, Hamilton fired at bomb throwing Turks, and directed attacks away from his section stationed in trenches behind him. Hamilton was only 19 years of age when he earned his VC citation. After World War1 ended, he became a butcher in the NSW town of Lithgow. Hamilton later attained the rank of Captain, when he served his country in World War 11 campaigns.

The happy-go-lucky and incredibly brave New Zealand born Captain Albert Shout of the 1st Battalion, received a posthumous VC award, after being KIA while leading bomb attacks on Turkish trenches.

On 9th August, 1915 Captain Shout led a small group in a charge down trenches which were manned by the enemy. The four bombs Shout threw killed eight Turkish soldiers, while the other enemy occupants fled from the trench. During the fierce action, Captain Shout lost both his right hand and left eye. He later died from his severe wounds, after being evacuated to a nearby hospital ship. Observers were awestruck by Shout's valour, with Private Thompson, from the 13th Battalion, describing his fellow Anzac's commitment as **"The bravest thing I ever saw"**.

Friends and family members maintain that war claimed the life of another Gallipoli VC winner in Lieutenant Hugo "Jim" Throssell, even though he was not actually KIA. This Tenth Light Horseman soldier gained a VC citation when he stayed with his men fighting off serious assaults, despite suffering severe wounds himself.

On his return to civilian life, Throssell worked as a farmer and real estate agent in Western Australia. He also became a socialist and an opponent of war, but finally lost an ongoing battle with depression. The 49 year old battle scarred veteran shot himself dead at his home, 14 years after World War 1 ended. Prior to his tragic ending, Throssell admitted that he "never recovered from his 1914-1918 war experiences". This belief was shared by the chaplain who conducted his funeral ceremony. The celebrant informed those present that

"He (Throssell) died for his country, as surely as if he had perished in the trenches".

Lieutenant Frederick Tubb, Corporal Alexander Burton and Corporal William Dunstan were all attached to the 7th Battalion. Tubb and Burton were both raised around Euroa in Victoria's north-east, and the two popular soldiers remained lifelong friends. The diminutive and extroverted Tubb was a grazier prior to enlisting, while Burton became an ironmonger, a church chorister and a keen local sportsman.

Burton, Tubb and Dunstan each gained

Captain Albert Shout

Lieutenant Hugo Throssell

Lieutenant
Frederick Tubb

Corporal
Alexander Burton

VCs, after continually defending a barricade they erected. Their sandbag defence needed to be reconstructed several times, after being demolished by enemy bombs. Burton was KIA by a sniper's bullet, and Dunstan was temporarily blinded in the same action. Tubb never recovered from serious wounds he sustained first at Gallipoli and later on the Western Front. He was 35 years of age when he died in September 1917.

William Dunstan's partial blindness lasted for almost a year, but the former messenger-boy for a Ballarat shopkeeper overcame his war injuries. In later years, Dunstan became highly successful in civilian life.

After being promoted to the rank of Lieutenant, Dunstan retired from the army in 1928. He later became General Manager of the Herald and Weekly Times Newspaper Group. William Dunstan was a very reserved man who shunned public recognition for his war achievements, but he became highly respected in business, judicial and parliamentary circles. A memorial erected in his honour still stands in Sturt Street Ballarat, while the "Dunstan VC Club" at Puckapunyal honours his name to this day.

John Simpson Kirkpatrick, one of Australia's most enduring legends from the 1915 Gallipoli campaign, is one of 13 candidates under current consideration for a post-humous VC award.

In April 2011, The Federal Government gave notice that the Defence Honours and Awards Appeals Tribunal would soon examine submissions, and conduct public hearings, which related to Simpson and the other nominees.

Lieutenant
William Dunstan

Kirkpatrick, a former itinerant labourer and trade union activist, joined the Australian Medical Corps at the advent of World War 1, using the name of John Simpson. His enlistment was mainly motivated by a wish to gain free passage back to his native England, and he was assigned the role of stretcher bearer after landing at Anzac Cove on 25th April, 1915.

Simpson obtained three local donkeys, dubbed "Murphy", "Abdul" and "Duffy". The group soon became a familiar sight, as they ferried dozens of wounded soldiers to safety from the heat of battle. The laconic Simpson was known to sing or whistle during the heroic rescue missions, and Indians fighting with the British forces, named him Badadur, or "bravest of the brave".

For 24 eventful days Simpson conducted his missions of mercy around war zones such as Shrapnel Gully and Monash Valley. The wounded soldiers he rescued would then be evacuated to hospital ships from the beach.

However on May 19th their daring missions

John Simpson
Kirkpatrick

C.E.W. Bean

ended, when Simpson, "Murphy" the donkey, and two wounded soldiers were fired upon by a Turkish soldier manning a machine gun. All three were killed, and the following inscription can still be observed on Simpson's grave at Anzac Cove's Beach Cemetery.

**"John Simpson Kirkpatrick
Served as Private J. Simpson
Australian Army Medical Corps
19/5/1915 Age 27.
"He gave his life that others may live".**

Charles Edwin Woodrow Bean, who was commonly referred to as C.E.W. Bean, became somewhat of a civilian hero in his role as a World War 1 correspondent. In his youth, his scholastic achievements in both Australia and England were most impressive, and after switching his occupation from law to journalism, C.E.W. Bean was appointed as the AIF's official war correspondent.

After Bean accompanied the Anzac's first convoy to Gallipoli, he gained the reputation of being a tireless, thorough and brave correspondent. Bean was nominated for a Military Cross, (MC), after rescuing a wounded soldier, but this recommendation was soon revoked. His rank as captain was not a military appointment, but an honorary position, which made him ineligible for the award. Unfortunately C.E.W. Bean's painstaking attention to detail became regarded as somewhat boring by Australian editors. Consequently, domestic newspapers began to print the shorter and more flamboyant articles provided by Ellis Ashmead-Bartlett, a well known British correspondent.

Bean, however, remained an influential and respected news source. He continued to provide war footage for almost the entire campaign, despite being wounded during the August offensive.

C.E.W. Bean attracted controversy in 1918, when he lobbied unsuccessfully against the decision to appoint Major Sir John Monash to the position of Commander of the Australian Corps. Anti-Semitism was then a common attitude in Australia, so to some extent, Bean was only mirroring the attitudes of many when he asserted that

"We do not want Australia represented by men, mainly because of their ability, natural and in-born in Jews, to push them-selves (to the forefront)."

To his credit, after Monash later guided Australian troops to an inspiring victory on the Western Front, C.E.W. Bean admitted his previous attitude had been improper. An apologetic Bean then praised the Australian commander for his wartime achievements.

C.E.W. Bean continued to provide insightful commentary during his tour of duty on the European war front. There, in France and Belgium, he observed first hand many examples of poor communication between commanders in the rear, and the troops on the front line. Bean memorably referred this major weakness as being the "fog of war".

On returning to Australia in 1919, Bean began the mammoth

task of compiling an Official History of World War 1. After two decades, the comprehensive and impressive war record was completed. Bean was 42 years of age when he married Ethel Young in 1921, and the couple later adopted a daughter.

The tireless Bean also played a vital role in establishing the prestigious Australian War Museum in Canberra, which remains a military collection icon for domestic and international visitors. Bean attended the official opening of the national monument on November 11th, 1941, and in 1952 he became Chairman of the Memorial Board.

C.E.W. Bean retained close ties with activities of the Australian War Museum, until he died in the Sydney suburb of Concord in his 88th year.

CHAPTER FOUR:

WESTERN FRONT WOES

After withdrawing from Gallipoli, many Australian soldiers were re-deployed to Europe's Western Front, which was a parallel line of defensive trenches and fortifications, stretching from the Belgian coast to the French-Swiss border.

Unremitting battles were waged there for three and a half years, and overall the World War 1 casualty rate on the Western Front has never been exceeded.

From March 1916, five Australian infantry divisions became involved in action in that area, and it was the 5th Division which first engaged the German enemy at the Battle of Fromelles.

It was a horrific conflict. A mammoth 5,533 soldiers were either killed or wounded on the first night. By 23rd July their comrades in the 1st Division suffered 5,286 losses after six days of bloody combat. To place the Western Front carnage in perspective, the casualty rate suffered at Fromelles and Pozieres was similar to the casualty rate experienced for the entire eight- month Gallipoli campaign.

A little over 60 years later, American singer-song writer Don McLean, composed "The Grave" in response to the Vietnam conflict. The extract from that song shown below, applied just as graphically to the traumatic war environment of the Western Front.

"And deep in the trench he waited for hours,
As he held to his rifle and prayed not to die...
But the silence of night was shattered by fire,
As guns and grenades blasted sharp through the air.
And one after another his comrades were slaughtered..."

The awful carnage of the Western Front continued. In the conflict at Pozieres, the casualty rate finally became 22,280 - a terrible sacrifice of young lives for the meaningless gain of 15 metres of enemy territory.

A scene from the Western Front

Only a kilometre away, at Moquet Farm, there were 6,300 casualties. It maintains grim memories for Australians to this very day, as more of our countrymen died on this small area of land than on any other battleground in the world. Overall, when the AIF withdrew from the Somme to re-organise their forces, 23,000 service personnel had been lost in only 45 days. By the end of 1916, the toll had grown to 42,000.

Western Front statistics continued to dwarf the enormous number of casualties suffered at Gallipoli. At the first Bullecourt battle on 11th April 1917, our troops were ordered to advance, without the assistance of any artillery support. Over 3,000 were lost and 1,170 captured. Less that a month later, the second Battle of Bullecourt resulted in the 1st, 2nd and 5th Divisions suffering 7,482 casualties.

The Western Front war scenes

In Belgium, between September and November of 1917, the Anzacs lost a mammoth 38,000 in just eight weeks at Menin Road, Polygon and Passchendale. In the air, the situation was even more hazardous: by 1918, for the first operational pilots, life expectancy was no more than three weeks.

On the ground, Western Front soldiers lived like rats behind sand bags and barbed wire, alongside dead and wounded

John Williamson

bodies covered in maggots and flies. In 1916-1917 the wettest winter for 36 years made ground conditions almost impassable, and reduced the trenches to stinking and disease riddled holes in the ground. In this featureless landscape of sticky mud, a condition known as "trench feet" became prevalent. It was a form of frost bite, which added even more discomfort to the soldiers on the front line.

From 1915, the horrors of gas warfare blinded, choked and burnt hundreds. Some of the victims never recovered, and, after the Great War ended, gas warfare was banned by the international community.

In total 333,000 served overseas in World War 1. The overall death rate from war injuries or disease exceeded 61,000, while over 150,000 suffered war injuries. Ultimately, the casualty rate among enlisted personnel, reached a staggering 65 percent.

What sustained our diggers in these months of grief and despair? Jingoistic and imperialistic ardour, which saw them first depart with "songs for the battle", soon passed its "used by date". Instead, it was a typically Australian sentiment called mateship, which helped many diggers through their darkest times.

Mateship is a difficult concept to define. To many in active service, mateship is the firm belief that your comrades in battle will do all that is humanly possible to protect your life. This unspoken mutual support helps sustain feelings of loyalty, endurance, courage and willingness to sacrifice, all of which are valued qualities within Australian military circles.

Mateship probably began in the Boer War. It was clearly evident among diggers in both World Wars, Korea and Vietnam, and it still prevails in Afghanistan today.

...True Blue, is it me and you?
Is it Mum and Dad?...
Is it standing by your mate... when he's in a fight?

The above extract forms part of the lyrics for "True Blue", a highly acclaimed song, which was composed by popular Australian singer-songwriter, John Williamson in 1981.

Being true blue equates closely with other Australian slang expressions, such as "fair dinkum" or "dinki-di". To Aussies, such terms applaud admirable qualities, such as honesty, trustworthiness and reliability, all of which are embraced in the concept of mateship.

The message of "True Blue" still resonates with many Australians. It was Steve Irwin's favourite song, and after this Australian environmental icon died tragically on September 4th 2006, John Williamson sang "True Blue" at his memorial service.

The armed forces certainly value the inspirational mateship message of this song. In October 2011, a veteran's group released a YouTube promotional video. The two songs used to enhance their message about the importance of Aussie mateship, were "I Am Australian" and "True Blue".

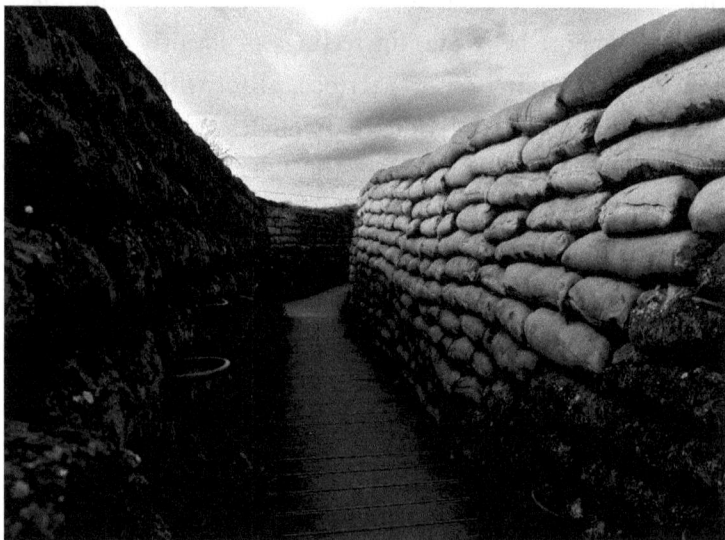

A Western Front War trench

Scenes of the Western Front today

CHAPTER FIVE:

A TRIFECTA OF OUTSTANDING COMMANDERS

Early in 1917, the Germans withdrew behind the Hindenburg Line, and during the following harrowing months, the tides of battle turned at last towards the Allies. In April, 1918 Aussie soldiers drove "the Huns" out of Villiers Bretonneau. By August the newly resurgent diggers, together with their Canadian comrades, seized Mt. St. Quentin. Morale began to flag in the German camp, as a "Messiah" named Monash began to strongly influence proceedings on the Western Front.

John Monash was born in 1865 to Jewish parents, who originated from Russia and Poland. In his youth he was a brilliant student, who gained Melbourne University degrees in Arts, Engineering and Law. Monash first became interested in military activities after completing his Engineering degree, and by 1914 he was Commander of the A.I.F.'s 4th Brigade in Egypt. It was there Monash experienced first hand, the negative effects which inevitably flow from incompetent command decisions.

General Sir
John Monash

In 1915 the 49 year old Monash received promotion at Gallipoli, but during the August offensive some observers criticised his performances as a Brigade Commander. Never-the-less, a year later on the Western front, (despite misgivings from influential war correspondent, C.E.W. Bean), John Monash was appointed as Major General of the 3rd Division.

His developing officer skills became evident in fierce confrontations at Messines, Ypres and Polygon Wood, and in May 1918, Monash was appointed Corps Commander of Australian forces. Bean was one former critic who warmed to his leadership potential, and he asserted that Monash was better suited to a Corps leadership position, than to Brigade responsibilities.

Bean's opinion may well have been accurate. In the Battle of Hamel, which became the first decisive Western Front victory for the Allies, it was Monash's skilful planning and attention to detail, which resulted in the town being captured. Victory at Hamel began a series of successful campaigns for the Australian General.

The innovative Monash became one of the first military leaders to co-ordinate different types of weaponry and defence. By using aeroplanes, tanks, bombing raids and ground troop attacks in rotation, he caused uncertainty and confusion in the opposition ranks. His often repeated common-sense advice was

" ...always have a plan. If it is not the best plan, it is as least better than no plan at all."

A recent biographer claimed that Monash was a man with "petrol in his veins, and a computer in his head". In combat he was certainly a meticulous planner, and nothing was left to chance in his preparations. Conferences were held with his fellow officers prior to the start of an offensive, where potential problems were discussed, and tactical plans formulated. Monash also firmly believed that commanders were responsible for the everyday welfare of troops under their command. Consequently he ensured that front line soldiers in the successful Hamel campaign received hot meals. Monash also catered for the logistical, medical and recreational needs of his troops.

Sir John Monash in civilian life

Furthermore, he rejected the British models of leadership, which produced so much carnage, both at Gallipoli and on the Western Front. Instead Monash maintained that.

"The true role of the infantry is not to expend itself on heroic physical effort, not to wither away under merciless machine-gun fire, not to impale itself on hostile bayonets...but to advance under the maximum protection of the maximum possible array of mechanical resources, in the form of guns, machine guns, tanks and aeroplanes;

to advance with as little impediment as possible."

Those surviving Australian soldiers, who previously experienced first hand the horrendous "cannon fodder" tactics favoured by some British military leaders, warmly embraced Monash's revolutionary and humane approach to warfare. Before mounting an enemy attack, the Australian general would bombard the enemy with gas and smoke shells. The Germans would then be forced to don gas masks. Gas attacks was abandoned by the Allies once ground forces were launched into the offensive, but continuing smoke bombs added to confusion and lack of visibility within enemy ranks.

The 150,000 Australian soldiers under Monash's command became inspired by his leadership. In 1918 a series of victories culminated with the German's Hindenburg Line being breached. Mont St. Quentin, which was previously considered to be impregnable, fell to the 2nd Division on August 8th, and this important gain was probably the turning point of the Western Front campaign. Monash was largely instrumental in gaining the victory, and he was knighted soon afterwards. Field-Marshall Bernard "Monty" Montgomery, Britain's revered military leader, was later moved to write that **"I would name Sir John Monash as the best General on the Western Front".**

Sir John Monash became prominent in civilian life after the war ended. He was appointed Vice Chancellor of Melbourne University and Head of the State Electricity Commission, (SEC). He was also strongly involved in Anzac Day commemorations and the Boy Scout movement. Monash University, the Monash Freeway and the Monash Medical Centre were all named after him, and his image appears on Australian $100 notes. Despite his fame, his modest tomb-stone at Brighton Cemetery in Melbourne only contains the inscription "John Monash". The high achiever's personal philosophy of life is summed up appropriately by the following statement ascribed to him.

Brigadier-General
Harry Elliott

"Adopt as your fundamental creed, that you will equip yourself for life, not solely for your own benefit, but for the benefit of the whole community".

Monash was 66 years of age when he passed away in 1931, and thousands of appreciative Australians paid him homage both at his funeral service and in the parade to his final resting place. Sir John Monash, (CCMG, KCB, and VD) was survived by his wife, Hannah, and their adopted daughter, Bertha.

**

Brigadier-General Harry Elliott was an Australian World War 1 officer, who attracted both high praise and criticism in military circles, during his controversial career. To the diggers who served under his command, Harry "Pompeii" Elliott was a hero. Officers in the British High Command, however, regarded the temperamental Australian, as being an ongoing nightmare.

Harry Elliott was the son of a Victorian

farmer. As a young man, he deferred his Law course at Melbourne University to volunteer for Boer War action. In South Africa Elliott was promoted to the rank of Corporal, and he was awarded a Distinguished Conduct Medal, (DSM). On returning home he completed his Law degree, and became a Lieutenant-Colonel, after enlisting in the AIF in 1904. A decade later, Elliott assumed command of the Australian Army, and he soon gained a reputation for imposing high standards of fitness and discipline. Harry Elliott was wounded and evacuated after the first landing at Gallipoli, but returned to action two months later.

Like Monash, Elliott displayed great attention to detail in combat situations. Early mornings in campaigns, saw him surveying battle fields where he was engaged, before finalising his tactics for the day. He displayed great trust in the judgements of subordinate officers, and he was passionately loyal to the men he commanded. Elliott was often brilliantly innovative in his military tactics, and appeared to revel in being exposed to dangerous situations.

On September 25th and 26th 1917, Elliott displayed excellent leadership at Polygon Wood, despite losing his brother, Captain G. C. Elliott, (MC), on that same Western Front battle ground. Harry Elliott also gained respect at Villiers Bretonneau, after leading a daring counter-attack on the enemy. Members of the 15th Brigade adored Elliott, and affectionately nick-named their commander "Pompeii".

His empathy for soldiers in front line action became obvious, when Fromelles on the Western Front was reduced to a killing field. One thousand four hundred and fifty-two members of Elliott's 15th Brigade were lost there. Survivors later discovered their devastated commander sobbing uncontrollably, when they returned to safety from the carnage. Elliott believed the tactics devised by the British officers, Brigadier-General Sir Brudenell White, and Brigadier-General Sir William Birdwood, were inhumane. He left the two military luminaries in no doubt about his dissatisfaction.

Despite his clashes with higher authority, Harry Elliott was awarded a DSO, but he "fell out" once more with White and Birdwood, after arresting a British staff officer for stealing a bottle of wine. Elliott was forced to release the highly miffed culprit. Soon after apparently less talented British officers gained divisional command positions, while "Pompeii" Elliott was overlooked. After stepping down from his command, he advised members of the 15th Brigade to **"...believe in themselves, Australia and the Almighty".**

Men who served under Harry Elliott continued to admire his forthrightness, his personal example, his generosity, and his refusal to waste lives on battlefields.

At first Elliott practised law, after returning to civilian life in Australia, before becoming a National Party Senator in Federal Parliament. By then he seemed obsessively bitter about his perceived war service grievances. He sometimes took embarrassing opportunities to air his displeasure about the British High Command, in inappropriate speeches to the Senate.

On 23rd May 1931, Harry Elliott died after receiving a bullet wound to the shoulder. He was found wounded soon after being treated in hospital for high blood pressure. Elliott died back in hospital shortly after being found wounded.. A subsequent inquest returned a suicide verdict, and may high ranking Australian army officers were among the pall bearers at his State funeral.

Harry Elliott was 53 when he died. He was survived by his wife, a daughter and a son.

"A cavalry raid attacked Bir el Abd, (near Beersheba), at the gallop over desert sand.

There was a sight! Four lines, crescent shaped, and over four miles long,

Going hell for leather!...I am a movie fan, and like westerns, but when I hear people getting all hot and bothered, when a mob of cowboys are galloping to the rescue, I cannot help but think...you never saw the charge at Bir el Abd!"(Post-war reminiscences of a former Light Horseman).

**

Harry Chauvel was first placed on a horse at the age of one, and he was later credited with commanding "the last great cavalry charge in history" near Beersheba, in North Africa, during World War 1.

Chauvel's upbringing, needs and personal motivation, fitted perfectly for a future soldier's career in the saddle. During his developmental years on the family farm in the Upper Clarence area of northern NSW, horses on the property were virtually treated like siblings.

They were also the main means of transport. Therefore, when seven year old Harry Chauvel commenced his education at Sydney Grammar School, a major part of the long journey for the young lad and his companions, was undertaken on horseback. In his final year of school, the diminutive 168 cm tall Chauvel became an accomplished jockey. He was 41 before he married, and his bride was 18 year old Sybil Jupp.

Harry Chauvel

Chauvel was in London, pursuing a career possibility with the UK War Office in 1914, when he assumed command of the 1st Light Horse Brigade. He was the first Australian born soldier, to be appointed to a command position.

In May1915, Chauvel's regiment relieved Monash's decimated 4th Brigade in Monash Valley. The Light Horse commander felt apprehensive, fearing his men's lack of experience in trench warfare would count against them. His misgivings proved to be accurate, but Harry Chauvel was unable to prevent the slaughter of many of his Light Horse troops. Only carnage resulted when Napoleonic era type bayonet charges were ordered by more highly ranked officers, such as Godley, Antill and Birdwood.

In the early months of 1916, Chauvel was appointed as Commander of the Mounted Division in North Africa. It was obvious his Light Horsemen units were far more suited to combat in a desert terrain, and in an early encounter they wrested Romani from the Turks.

The conflict pitted 1,500 Horsemen against nearly 25,000 enemy soldiers, so tactics played a vital role in the outcome. With his numerically inferior forces, Chauvel cleverly juggled his offensive and defensive strategies. He correctly forecast where the Turks would mount their major attack, and placed his communications and defence networks accordingly. Success depended on his men maintaining their position, until British reinforcements arrived in early August.

At 10am on August 4th, the Australians engaged the Turks in hand to hand combat. The first hour was like Lone Pine revisited, and by early next morning the enemy made inroads. It was then that Chauvel activated the 500 strong 2nd Light Horse Brigade, which he had held back in reserve. The dehydrated and exhausted Turks were shocked, when fresh reinforcements arrived at daybreak.

A fierce battle raged for at least five hours, before British reinforcements arrived at 8pm. After two Turkish battalions surrendered, Romani was saved.

"It was the empty Turkish water bottle that won the battle," a relieved Chauvel later claimed.

The Romani battle was also the first British-shared victory in the North African campaign, and provided fresh hope that the enemy would ultimately be expelled from the Western Desert and Middle East regions.

By then Chauvel's calm decision making, and continual encouragement, had won the support of the troops. Victory at Romani was followed by success at Wellington Ridge, when the enemy was chased back to swamp lands near Katia. Before long the Anzac's western desert casualty rate was 203 dead and 80 wounded, but by then the Turks had lost close to 25,000 soldiers.

These statistics indicated Chauvel was not interested in unnecessary combats; the welfare of his troops and horses remained of paramount importance. He once explained his command beliefs in the following terms.

"Light Horse must have all the features of fighting infantry, cavalry and the raider. They must have both terrifying force and the capacity to fade like ghosts".

These qualities came to the fore in 1916 pre-Christmas battles, when Wadi El Arish and Magdhaba fell to the Allies. Chauvel only lost 22 men in these skirmishes, and nearly 1,300 enemy prisoners were taken. Following these successes, he was officially recognised, receiving a Knight Commander of St. Michael and St. George, (KCMG), award. Four months later Sir Harry Chauvel became the first officer from a Dominion force to be promoted to the rank of Corps Commander.

Capturing Beersheba became the next mission, and by 31st October, Chauvel's men were ready to attack the town. The outskirts of the settlement were breached, but the Allies urgently needed water from Beersheba's wells to remain viable.

Before darkness fell, approximately 800 members of the 4th and 12th Light Horse Regiments, sartorially dressed in emu plumes, bandoliers and spurs, made their famous cavalry charge. Once enemy machine guns were negated, infantry soldiers prevented the enemy from destroying most of the water wells. Victory at Beersheba, where Sir Harry Chauvel unleashed the most potent cavalry force ever seen, was his finest wartime achievement.

After Turkey surrendered, Chauvel returned to Australia.

He accepted the role of Inspector General of the AIF until his retirement in 1930, and he also frequently led annual Anzac parade marches.

Chauvel's talented children led interesting lives. One of his daughters, who became Elyne Mitchell, later wrote the famous Silver Brumby series of books. In 1938 Elyne also won the Canadian downhill skiing championships. Another daughter, Eve, was marooned at sea for hours during World War 11, and Chauvel's two sons at one time served with the Cavalry Regiment of the British Indian Army.

His nephew, Charles Chauvel, directed the popular films "Jedda" and "Forty Thousand Horsemen". The main theme of the latter movie was the famous cavalry charge which was led by his famous uncle.

During World War11, Sir Harry Chauvel, (CCMG, KCB), headed the VDC, which was similar to Britain's Home Guard defence unit, He remained active at Melbourne's Victoria Barracks, until he died in March 1945 at the age of 79.

Melbourne's Victoria Barracks

CHAPTER SIX:

WARRIORS OF THE WESTERN FRONT

More than 50 VCs were awarded to Australian servicemen involved in Western Front battles. This large number of honoured heroes, from just one theatre of war, speaks volumes for the extreme bravery they displayed. It also demonstrates the huge dangers all Western front warriors faced, during the 42 month duration of that dreadful conflict.

The Australian VC winners from the Western Front are listed below in alphabetical order. Brief citation details relating to their achievements, as well as some individual biographical details, are included.

Lance Corporal Thomas Leslie Axford (1894-1983): Axford was attached to the 16th Battalion. In Hamel Woods, France, his group came under heavy German fire as they advanced up a slope. An adjoining platoon suffered heavy casualties.

Axford rushed to their assistance, jumping into an enemy trench and bayoneted or bombed machine gun crews. Ten Germans were killed and six captured.

Lance Corporal
Thomas Leslie
Axford

Private Robert
Matthew Beatham

He then checked on the group which had been delayed, before returning to his own platoon. Lance Corporal Axford and other Diggers then laid out more assault line tapes, only ten metres from enemy positions.

Axford was born in Carrieton in South Australia. In civilian life he was a clerk and a businessman, and Tom Axford was 89 years of age when he died in Perth.

Private Robert Matthew Beatham (1894-1918): A member of the 18th Battalion, which became involved in fierce combat, on 9th August 1918, at Rosieres near Villers-Bretonneau, France.

Robert Beatham was born in England, and he was 20 years of age when he relocated to Australia. It appears Beatham was "a bit of a lad" during his AIF years. He was sent back to Australia as a disciplinary measure early in World War 1. Months later, on New Years Eve, when he was stationed in England, Beatham was found guilty of being absent without leave. For this offence, the young rogue was fined, and he was also assigned special field punishment duties.

By then Robert Beatham had been wounded twice during active combat situations, and his actions on 9th August 1918, proved he was an extremely brave soldier.

On that day, when the 8th Division was delayed by enemy fire, Beatham and Lance-Corporal Nottingham bombed and fought the German foe, killing ten and capturing at least another ten.

Two days later, the English born Beatham was KIA, when he attempted to overcome another machine gun defence. He died at the age of 24.

2ND Lieutenant Frederick Birks (1894-1917):

2nd Lieutenant
Frederick Birks

Welsh born Fred Birks arrived in Australia at the age of 19. This adventurous young man, who loved vigorous sports such as boxing, was first employed as a labourer and a waiter in various parts of Tasmania, Victoria and South Australia, before enlisting in the AIF.

Birks was assigned to the 6th Battalion. On 20th September 1917, at Glencorse Wood near Ypres in Belgium, a corporal and he rushed a German pill box to delay an enemy advance. The Germans present were killed, and the pill box was captured.

They then overcame another 25 enemy soldiers, wounding nine and capturing the other 16.

On the following day, Fred Birks was KIA in a bombing attack, when he attempted to rescue fellow comrades. He was then 23 years of age.

Lieutenant Arthur
Seaford Blackburn

Lieutenant Arthur Seaford Blackburn (1892-1960): Arthur Blackburn graduated in Law from the University of Adelaide in 1913, and at the age of 21 he enlisted in the "fighting 10th Battalion". This group was among the first Anzacs to land at Gallipoli, and Blackburn was promoted to the position of 2nd Lieutenant during the arduous campaign.

Blackburn was 23 years of age when the 10th Battalion became involved in heavy action at Pozieres in France on 23rd July, 1916. In the fierce battle, Blackburn personally led four successive bombing raids which destroyed much enemy resistance, and gained 350 metres of enemy territory.

Shortly after receiving his VC award, the newly married Arthur Blackburn was discharged from military service on medical grounds. He resumed his legal career, and became an active campaigner for the pro-conscription movement. Between 1918 and 1921 Arthur Blackburn was the National Party Member for Sturt in the South Australian Parliament, and he was also prominent in the state's Soldier's Sailor's and Airmen's League.

Arthur Blackburn returned to active service when World War 11 began, and this much decorated soldier unfortunately became a Japanese Prisoner of War (POW) for three years.

Arthur Seaford Blackburn (VC, CMG,

CBE, ED) was born in Adelaide, South Australia. He was aged 68 when he died in the city of his birth.

Lieutenant Albert Borella (1881-1968): An officer with the 26th Battalion, which became engaged in battle on 17th and 18th July 1918, at Villers Bretonneau in France.

Lieutenant Albert Borella

Despite being heavily outnumbered, Borella shot two enemy machine gun operators with his revolver, while leading his platoon in a trench engagement. In another assault his group captured 30 enemy soldiers.

Albert Borella was 37 years of age when he was awarded his VC - the oldest World War1 recipient to gain the honour.

There is no doubting Borella's determination to volunteer for war action. In his youth, when Australia first became involved in World War 1 action, Albert Borella was employed as a cook at Tennant Creek. His attempts to enlist in the army failed, as the government of the day did not accept applicants from the Northern Territory (NT).

Borella remained undaunted by the setback. He trekked over rough country in stifling heat, (and at times swam across flooded rivers), for at least 88 kilometres, before sailing from Darwin to Townsville. When Borella finally arrived in the Queensland port city, he was allowed to volunteer for active service.

After returning from the Western Front, Albert Borella farmed near the Victorian town of Hamilton, and he gained local pre-selection with the National Party for a State election. He later settled in the NSW border city of Albury, where family members live to this day.

Borella is remembered as a modest man, who spoke little about his experiences in both world wars. The Army Logistics Training Centre, at nearby Bandiana, named their Soldiers Club the Borella VC Club in his honour.

Albert Borella was born at Borung near Bendigo, and he lived until the age of 87. Borella, VC, is now buried in the Presbyterian section of the North Albury cemetery. Borella Road in Albury, still honours the name of this reticent war hero.

Corporal Walter Thomas Ernest Brown

Corporal Walter Thomas Ernest Brown (1885-1942): Served with the 20th Battalion. On 6th July 1918, at Villers Bretonneau, France, Brown's advance party came under sniper fire, after they seized an enemy trench. Brown collected two small bombs and charged towards the Germans, despite being subjected to heavy fire. He felled one enemy soldier with his fist, and used bomb threats to force the surrender of another 12.

During World War 11, the then 54 year old

Brown re-enlisted, after convincing authorities he was only 39. The intrepid war veteran was later KIA in Singapore. Brown's death occurred, when he defiantly walked towards armed Japanese soldiers with grenades in hand, and shouted "No surrender for me!"

His body was never recovered. Tom Brown was born in New Norfolk, Tasmania, and today a memorial plaque honours his name, in the NSW town of Leeton.

Temporary Corporal Alexander Henry Buckley (1891-1918): He was assigned to the 54th Battalion, which became involved in dangerous conflict at Peronne, France between 1st and 2nd September, 1918.

Temporary Corporal Alexander Henry Buckley

In rainy conditions on 1st September, Temporary Corporal Buckley's battalion attempted to break through a German position, between Mont St Quentin and Peronne.

The group overcame heavy artillery fire, and secured the first line of enemy trenches, before being thwarted by a nest of German machine guns. Buckley and a comrade defied the odds and rushed forward, shooting four men, and taking 22 others captives in their surprise attack.

The Germans retreated across the Peronne Bridge, before destroyed that main entrance into town. The only entry point remaining was a footbridge, which was well defended by machine guns. Buckley was one of four who tried to access the town via the footbridge, but he was KIA during the brave attempt.

Alex Buckley was born in the NSW town of Warren, where he became a farmer. He was aged 27 when he died at Peronne.

Sergeant Maurice Vincent Buckley, Alias Gerald Sexton (1891-1922): While serving with the 13th Battalion at Le Verquier in France, Sergeant Buckley used his gun to effectively clear enemy troops. He later shot a German machine gun crew, while being fired on himself by machine guns. Buckley retaliated with mortar fire, to put an enemy trench out of action. By the end of the day Buckley was credited with capturing 100 prisoners.

Sergeant Maurice Vincent Buckley

Buckley was a colourful character who never married, but his short life was indeed eventful. He assumed his mother's maiden name of "Sexton", after being previously discharged as a deserter, under his legal name of "Buckley". The sentence was imposed, after Maurice Buckley deserted from a Langwarrin army training camp in March, 1916. Later he disclosed his real name, when King George V presented him with his VC award, at Buckingham Palace in London.

After returning to Australia, Buckley

opposed moves to legislate conscription for war service. He led a group of 10,000 in a Melbourne march, a protest which had been sanctioned by the Catholic Archbishop, Daniel Mannix.

The flamboyant Maurice Buckley was only 29 years of age when he was badly injured in a horse riding accident, after being dared to jump over a railway gate. Buckley died 12 days later, and ten other VC winners were pall bearers at his funeral. He is now buried in Melbourne's Brighton Cemetery.

Private Patrick Joseph Bugden (1897-1917): He was a member of the 31st Battalion, and his brave actions were noted at Polygon Wood in Belgium, between the 26th and 28th September, 1917.

Private Patrick Joseph Bugden

Bugden twice attacked a strong German pill box position with bombs, and forced the occupants to surrender at bayonet point. He also saved a corporal from three Germans, as well as rescuing comrades who were wounded, on at least five occasions.

Patrick Bugden was only 20 years of age when he was KIA on 28th September, 1917. Bugden Avenue in Canberra was named in his honour.

Private John Carroll

Private John Carroll (1891-1971): A soldier attached to the 33rd Unit. Between June 7th and 10th June 1917, at Messines in Belgium, Carroll bravely attacked enemy trenches. He bayoneted three Germans, rescued a comrade, and took command of a machine gun. Over the entire four days of bitter conflict, Private Carroll rescued two other comrades, and he continued to display fearless courage.

Carroll is remembered as being a casual, "happy go lucky" type person, who was affectionately nicknamed "the wild Irishman". He was born in Brisbane, and after the war concluded, Carroll unfortunately had a foot amputated from a work related accident.

John Carroll was aged 80 when he died in Perth.

Private George Cartwright

Private George Cartwright (1894-1978): He was also a member of the 33rd Battalion. On 31st August 1917, near Peronne in France, Private Cartwright was with two companies, who were thwarted in their advance by withering machine gun fire.

The English born Cartwright rushed forwards, threw a bomb at the post, and then captured both the machine gun and nine prisoners. His gallantry was applauded by his cheering comrades, and the inspired group fought on with renewed vigour.

Prior to World War 1, George Cartwright worked as a farm labourer in the Elsmore district of NSW. After the war he became a motor mechanic, and later an assistant cashier in Sydney. He died in the Sydney suburb of Epping at the age of 84. George Cartwright was survived by his second wife and a son from his first marriage.

Sergeant Claud Charles Castleton (1893-1916): He was from the Unit 5 Machine Gun Company. Castleton's brave actions were recognised at Pozieres on 28th July, 1916.

Sergeant Castleton twice rescued wounded comrades, despite being endangered by heavy machine gun fire. The English born VC was KIA, after being shot in the back while attempting a third rescue mission. He died at the age of 23.

Sergeant Claud Charles Castleton

Castleton Crescent in Canberra was named in his honour.

Captain Percy Henry Cherry (1895-1917): Cherry was a member of the 26th Battalion, and he was awarded a VC for his heroism at Lagnicourt in France on 27th March, 1917.

Captain Cherry unexpectedly found himself in command, after his unit's officers were either killed or wounded. Cherry then led his men in a successful assault of the village.

Captain Percy Henry Cherry

He then strongly defended the area, using a Lewis gun, rifles and grenades.

Despite being wounded on the morning of the fierce battle, Captain Cherry refused to leave his post. That afternoon, the 22 year old hero was KIA.

Percy Cherry was born in Drysdale on Victoria's Bellarine Peninsula, but moved with his family to Tasmania at the age of seven. In the island state, Cherry became both an excellent apple picker and a fine marksman. Before the advent of war, Percy Cherry trained as a drill instructor.

Just weeks before he was killed, a 21 year old Cherry was awarded a Maltese cross, (MC), after his party captured two machine gun posts. Previously, on 5th August 1916, Captain Cherry mortally wounded a German officer. However, in that same incident on the Somme, Cherry was badly injured himself, when both soldiers fired simultaneously at each other.

The dying German passed on some letters for Cherry to post, which he did while recuperating from his own wounds in England.

In recent years, a street in Drysdale was named after Captain Percy Cherry.

Private Thomas Cooke

Private Thomas Cooke (1881-1916): Cooke was a member of the 8th Battalion, and his special act of valour occurred at Pozieres France, between 24th and 25th July, 1916.

The New Zealand born Cooke displayed great heroism, before he, together with 80 members of the Lewis gun team in his battalion, were all KIA. Tom Cooke was 25 years of age, when he was found dead beside his gun.

Private William Matthew Currey (1895-1948): He was a member of the 53rd Battalion, and on 1st September 1918, at Mont St Quentin in France, the group encountered heavy artillery fire.

Private William Matthew Currey

Despite the inherent danger, Currey rushed forward, killed an entire German gun crew, and captured a machine gun. He repeated that brave action on the afternoon of the same day, when he again inflicted heavy casualties on enemy forces. Early next morning Currey overcame the effects of gas inhalation, and successfully guided a company to safety.

William Currey was born in Wallsend, NSW. In civilian life, he worked as a labourer and railway worker, and for seven years he served as the state Labor Member for Kogarah. Bill Currey passed away in Sydney, at the age of 53.

Private Henry Dalziel (1893 1965): Dalziel was a member of the 15th Battalion, which was involved in action at Hamel Wood in France

Private Henry Dalziel

on 4th July, 1918.

After helping a comrade thwart enemy machine gun fire, Dalziel dashed forward. Using only a revolver, he killed or captured the crew of an enemy post. This important gain allowed an advance group to proceed further.

Dalziel continued firing his gun throughout the battle, despite losing the tip of his trigger finger.

Henry Dalziel was born at Irvine Bank in Queensland, and later became a railway fireman as well as a song writer. Dalziel was troubled by war injuries for much of his life, and he was aged 72 when he died in Brisbane.

Corporal Phillip Davey

Corporal Phillip Davey (1896-1953): Davey was assigned to the 10th Battalion, which participated in active duty at Merris in France on 28th June, 1918.

Corporal Davey attacked an enemy machine gun post, after his commanding officer was KIA. Acting alone, he used grenades to negate approximately 60% of the enemy position, before returning to his unit to replenish his supply of grenades. These weapons were used to kill the remaining eight enemy combatants, which allowed Davey to control the gun position. He was then able to repel enemy counter attacks with the machine gun, before being wounded. Corporal Davey was then withdrawn from the conflict.

Phillip Davey was born in Goodwood South Australia. At various times he worked as a horse driver and railway signalman, and endured poor health for many years from his war experiences. He was aged 57, when he died in Adelaide.

Sergeant John James Dwyer (1890-1962): Dwyer was a member of the 4th Machine Gun Company Unit, which was involved in active duty at Zonnebeke in Belgium on 26th September, 1917.

Sergeant John James Dwyer

Sergeant Dwyer was in charge of a Vickers machine gun. He rushed forward to success-fully negate the enemy's machine gun post, and killed all the German soldiers manning the position. Two guns were then used by Dwyer to oppose subsequent counter attacks, and the enemy suffered further casualties. The brave sergeant continued to be effective, when the battle continued next day.

In 1931 John Dwyer became a parliamen-tarian in his home state of Tasmania, and between August 1958 and May 1959, he served as Deputy Premier. John Dwyer was still an elected member, when he died in Hobart at the age of 72.

Lieutenant Alfred Edward Gaby

Lieutenant Alfred Edward Gaby (1892-1918): This officer was attached to the 28th Battalion. Lieutenant Gaby was posthumously nominated for a VC, following his heroic actions at Villers Bretonneau on 8th August 1918.

The company Gaby commanded was pinned down by heavy enemy fire. He broke the stalemate by singlehandedly approaching a strong point of the German defence. Gaby then ran along the parapet firing his revolver at the gunners. The enemy was driven from their machine guns, and forced to surrender. Four machine guns were confiscated in the brave assault.

Three days later Lieutenant Alfred Gaby was KIA from sniper fire. He was 26 years of age, and had previously been a farmer in his home state of Tasmania.

Lance Corporal Bernard Sidney Gordon

Lance Corporal Bernard Sidney Gordon (1891-1963): Gordon was assigned to the 41st Battalion at Fargny Wood near Bray in France, on 27th August, 1918.

When his Battalion was wedged in an awkward position, Lance-Corporal Gordon acted alone to attack a dangerous German machine gun post. He killed their gunner, and later captured an enemy officer and ten other soldiers.

The Lance-Corporal then entered Fargny

Wood, and cleared an enemy trench. In this foray, 29 prisoners and two machine guns were obtained. Further trenches also surrendered, with 22 POWs and three additional machine guns being added to Gordon's booty.

After returning to civilian life, the Tasmanian born Bernie Gordon became a dairy farmer. He fathered nine children, before dying in Brisbane at the age of 72.

Captain Robert Cuthbert Grieve (1889-1957): He was a member of the 37th Battalion, which was involved in active duty at Messines in Belgium, on 7th June, 1917.

Captain Robert
Cuthbert Grieve

After 50% of his group were slain by artillery fire from a German pill box, Captain Grieve cautiously approached the enemy post. He threw Mills bombs into shell holes, which stopped the gunner's fire from his trench. Captain Grieve then killed all the other occupants in the pill box, by rolling two other bombs through a firing slit. His company was then able to occupy the trench, but Grieve was badly wounded by sniper fire.

The gallant captain was evacuated first to England and then Australia, while he recovered from acute trench nephritis and double pneumonia. Grieve later married Nurse May Bowman, who cared for him throughout his long recuperation.

Robert Grieve was born in the Melbourne bay side suburb of Brighton. He later became managing director of a soft goods warehouse. After suffering a heart attack, he died at the age of 68, and now lies at rest in the Presbyterian section of the Springvale Crematorium.

Corporal Arthur Charles Hall

Corporal Arthur Charles Hall: (1896-1958): Hall was attached to the 54th Battalion at Peronne in France, on 1st and 2nd September 1918, when his VC award was gained.

While under attack, Hall singlehandedly rushed a machine gun post. He killed four enemy soldiers, forced another 15 to surrender, and seized two machine guns. After covering the advance of the rest of his unit, Corporal Hall captured other small posts, and confiscated enemy weapons.

The bridge into Peronne was crossed next day before being destroyed, and the enemy was cleared from the area. Hall also carried a badly wounded comrade to a medical care area.

Arthur Hall was born in Sydney, and he later became a commercial traveller in the soft goods trade. He died in the NSW town of West Bogan, at the age of 82.

Corporal George Julian Howell

Corporal George Julian Howell (1893-1964): George "Snowy" Howell was employed as a builder before he enlisted for army service in June 1915. On 6th May 1917, Corporal Howell was serving with the 1st Battalion at Bullecourt in France, when his group was driven back by flame throwers. The 3rd Brigade hero then committed his unit to withstand fierce attacks that followed.

Corporal Howell's reaction was to run along the top of a parapet dropping bombs into enemy trenches, which forced the Germans to scurry to safety. Once his bomb supply was exhausted, Howell continued to pursue the enemy with a bayonet charge, until he was severely wounded.

"Snowy" Howell was born in Enfield NSW. He settled in the Sydney suburb of Coogee, after recovering from his war injuries, and worked for many years in advertising sections of several newspapers. George "Snowy" Howell was aged 71 when he died in Perth.

Lieutenant George Mawby Ingram (1889-1961): This officer was attached to the 24th Battalion, when his brave deeds were officially recognised on 5th October 1918, near Peronne in France.

Ingram's platoon, despite being under heavy sniper fire, succeeded in capturing nine machine guns and killing 42 enemy soldiers. Lieutenant Ingram assumed command, after the Company Commander was wounded.

Lieutenant George Mawby Ingram

Under his leadership, six more Germans were killed and another machine gun obtained.

The 24th Battalion's success continued, with 62 more POWs being taken into confinement, once their machine gun operator was removed.

George Ingram, (VC, MC), was born in Bendigo, and prior to the war he was a building contractor. On returning to civilian life, Ingram worked as a foreman, and during World War 11 he served as a Captain with the Royal Australian Engineers.

George Ingram married three times, and two of his wives were previously widows. Two sons were born from his last two marriages. George Ingram was aged 72, when he died in Hastings, from a coronary vascular condition.

Private Reginald Roy Inwood

Private Reginald Roy Inwood (1890-1971) was born in Adelaide, but his family soon moved to Broken Hill, where Roy Inwood began his working life in the local mines. Two of his siblings also enlisted in the army with Roy, and his 20 year old brother, Robert, was KIA on the Western Front at Pozieres in July 1916.

Roy Inwood became assigned to the 10th Battalion, and he displayed considerable courage in a battle at Polygon Wood, in

Belgium, on 20th and 21st September, 1917. In a remarkable solo effort, Private Inwood captured nine prisoners and killed several more, who were occupying a strong enemy post. Inwood's brave actions enabled his battalion to advance and consolidate their position. Later Private Inwood, who feared a German counter attack that night, volunteered his services for a reconnaissance patrol of the danger area. Next morning Inwood bombed a machine gun area. The only enemy survivor soon surrendered.

After World War 1 ended, Roy Inwood returned briefly to Broken Hill, before working in various manual occupations in Tasmania, and on Kangaroo Island. His first marriage ended in divorce, his second wife died, and after marrying a third time, Roy Inwood returned permanently to Adelaide. There he was employed by the Adelaide City Council for the last 27 years of his working life. Roy Inwood was aged 81 when he died in his home city.

Private John William Alexander Jackson (1897-1959): Bill Jackson was born into a large family near the NSW town of Gunbar, a district where he was later employed as a farm labourer.

Private John William Alexander Jackson

After enlisting in the AIF, Bill Jackson was assigned to the 17th Battalion. Before long,

81

Private Jackson's bravery in trench warfare near Armentieres, on 25th and 26th June 1916, deservedly received special recognition.

Following his safe delivery of a German prisoner, Private Jackson returned to "no man's land" from where he brought back a wounded comrade, while under heavy enemy fire. Jackson's arm was nearly blown off during his brave rescue mission, and severe pain caused him to lapse into unconsciousness, after his mate and he reached safety. Later, despite his terrible injuries, John Jackson returned to his group, before embarking on another successful rescue mission. His mutilated arm was later amputated.

After hostilities ceased, the shy and reticent young man was overwhelmed by the hero's welcome he received on his return to Gunbar. His amputation caused him to reject the generous offer of a farm in his home area, and Bill Jackson mostly sold animal skins to earn a living, before marrying Ivy Morris in 1932. The union produced a daughter, and the family moved to Melbourne in 1953, where Bill was employed by the Melbourne City Council for six years, before dying at the age of 61.

In May 2008, Bill Jackson's VC medal was privately sold. It is rumoured that this highly esteemed item of war memorabilia was purchased for the relatively cheap price of $650,000.

Captain Clarence Smith Jeffries (1894-1917): was born in the Newcastle suburb of Wallsend, and became he a surveyor with a mining company after completing his secondary school education. During his short life of 23 years, Clarrie

Jeffries was remembered as being a useful local cricketer, and a keen horseman. In 1912 he joined a militia battalion, and once war broke out in 1914, Jeffries was assigned to the 34th Battalion.

His unit became involved in active duty at Passchendaele, Belgium, on 12th October, 1917. It was there that Captain Jeffries was confronted by two German pill boxes. He organised a bombing attack, which caused 25 enemy troops to surrender, and two machine guns to be confiscated. Jeffries, and a group of 12 soldiers, then captured another 30 Germans, while further machine guns were also seized.

Unfortunately Captain Clarence Jeffries was KIA during the battle.

Captain Clarence Smith Jeffries

Private Jorgen Christian Jensen (1891-1922): was born in Loegstoer, Denmark, and he immigrated to Australia when he was 18 years of age. Joergen Jensen became a British subject on 7th September 1914. After enlisting in the AIF, Private Jensen was attached to the 50th Battalion, which saw combat at Noreuil in France, on 2nd April, 1917.

At 5.30am on April 2nd 1917, the 50th and 51st Battalions attacked a German outpost village. Private Jensen was attached to a party which stormed a strong barricade. Jensen threw one

Private Jorgen Christian Jensen

bomb into the German group. He then used his teeth to withdraw the pin from another missile, as he boldly advanced on the enemy.

The enemy troops were stopped in their tracks by this unexpected development. Private Jensen induced the frightened men to surrender, by convincing them they were "surrounded" by allied forces. He then persuaded one of the prisoners to implore another group of Germans to give themselves up.

By that stage, the Australian battalions came under threat from "friendly enemy fire", so the daring Jensen stood up on the barricade, and waved his helmet at his comrades, until the firing ceased. The prisoners were then escorted back to safety.

After the war ended Joergen Jensen worked at the Truro Hotel in South Australia, where the manager was a married woman who had two daughters. Her name was Katy Herman, and she later divorced her husband and married Joergen Jensen. The newlyweds moved to Adelaide, where Jensen became employed as a marine store dealer. Unfortunately he continued to be troubled by serious war injuries, and Joergen Jensen was only 31 years of age, when he died in Adelaide in 1922.

Lieutenant William Donovan Joynt

Lieutenant William Donovan Joynt (1889-1986): This officer with the 8th Battalion, rendered outstanding service at Herleville Wood near Chuignes in France, on 23rd August, 1918.

Lieutenant Joynt reorganised a 6th Battalion unit, which had lost its officers in battle. He urged them forward, and the group captured a German post and 50 prisoners.

Then battalion members moved to within 50 metres of an enemy machine gun post. They captured the leader of an advance party and his group at pistol point,

before forcing the remaining German troops out of the woods. Joynt was wounded in the fierce three-day battle which followed.

In his youth Bill Joynt was a restless individual who worked in a variety of occupations, including office duties, soldiering and farming. He then became a printer and publisher for over 60 years.

Bill Joynt remained a bachelor until the age of 43. He stayed active in local government matters in Berwick to the south-east of Melbourne. Then, after he and his wife, Edith, purchased artist Tom Robert's house in Kallista, Joynt became the author of three books.

Edith died in 1978. The Brighton-born William Joynt, VC, survived her for a further eight years, before he died at the age of 97, in the Melbourne suburb of Windsor.

Private Thomas James Bede Kenny (1896-1953) became a chemist's assistant in the Sydney suburb of Bondi, after matriculating from his secondary college. He enlisted in the AIF shortly after World War 1 began, and became attached to the 2nd Battalion, which saw fierce action at Hermes in France, on 9th April, 1917.

Private Thomas
James Bede Kenny

Private Bede Kenny's platoon came under heavy machine gun fire, which caused heavy casualties. He singlehandedly forced the enemy to retreat, and killed a German soldier who obstructed him. Kenny then activated three bombs, with the last missile destroying the German post.

When his platoon arrived at the scene, Kenny had forced the surrender of the post survivors, and he was in total control of the situation.

After returning to Australia, Bede Kenny mostly worked as a commercial traveller. At the age of 31 he married a Sydney florist, and Kenny and his wife Kathleen produced three children. Two of his offspring died prematurely after contacting rheumatic fever, and those close to the family, believed Bede Kenny never recovered from these tragedies.

Over the years, Bede Kenny said little about his war experiences, but he suffered constantly from the effects of trench feet. Kenny also battled with partial deafness, and he was only 57-years-of-age when he died in Sydney.

Private John Leak (1892-1972): was attached to the 9th Battalion, which became locked in combat at Pozieres, France, on 23rd July, 1916.

Despite being under heavy enemy fire, the English-born Private Leak ran forward and

Private John Leak

threw three bombs into the German post. He then bayoneted three enemy soldiers, and defiantly retaliated with bombs, before he was forced to retreat quickly to safety, after being badly gassed.

John Leak appeared to suffer both physical and mental scars from his war experiences. He mostly worked in Western Australia as a garage proprietor, and was aged 80 when he passed away in Adelaide.

Sergeant Albert David Lowerson (1896-1945): Alby Lowerson was working as a gold prospector before enlisting in the AIF. He saw active service with the 21st Battalion, which became involved in armed combat at Mont St. Quentin near Peronne in France, on 1st September, 1918.

Sergeant Albert David Lowerson

After being pinned down by enemy artillery, Sergeant Lowerson organised a storming party of seven, which succeeded in capturing 30 German soldiers and confiscating 12 machine guns. Then, despite suffering a wound to the thigh, Lowerson ensured the post was consolidated, and the dispersal of prisoners was organised.

Albert Lowerson was born in the Victorian town of Myrtleford. He later died prematurely at the age of 49 in his home town..

Private Robert
Mactier

Private Robert Mactier (1890-1918): was a soldier with the 23rd Battalion, which saw action at Mont St. Quentin, France, on 1st September, 1918.

Private Mactier acted as a runner during a fierce engagement. In this capacity, he ran to an enemy barricade, lobbed a bomb into the enclosure, and killed eight Germans with bombs or his revolver.

Mactier then threw the barricade's machine gun off the parapet, before forcing the surrender of a second garrison, which contained six of the enemy. A third garrison was also destroyed. Tragically, when Private Mactier was throwing bombs into a fourth garrison, he was shot dead by machine gun fire.

Robert Mactier was born in the Victorian town of Tatura, where he worked on the family farm, before enlisting for war service. Mactier was aged 28, when he was KIA.

Lieutenant Joseph
Maxwell

Lieutenant Joseph Maxwell (1896-1967): was an officer with the 18th Battalion, which was involved in combat near Estes, France, on 3rd October 1918.

After his company commander was badly wounded, Lieutenant Maxwell assumed command. On reaching heavily fortified wire, Maxwell singlehandedly captured the most dangerous German gun position. During this attack, he killed three of the enemy group, and captured a further four.

His brave solo actions allowed the remainder of his company to join him. Maxwell then took over another machine gun position, before being temporarily captured. However the resilient Lieutenant shot two of his captors, and escaped with another two Germans, whom he had previously captured.

After the war ended Joseph Maxwell became the author of a popular book titled "Hell's Bells and Mademoiselles". The rough, tough boiler maker from Forest Lodge NSW worked in many occupations, before he died in Sydney at the age of 71.

Lieutenant Lawrence (Laurence) Douglas "Fats" McCarthy (1892-1975): was attached to the 16th Battalion, which saw action at Madame Wood in France on 23rd August, 1918.

Lieutenant Lawrence Douglas McCarthy

After his group's advance was thwarted by heavy machine gun fire, McCarthy and Sergeant Robbins, (DCM, MM), broke the deadlock decisively. The pair captured four machine gun positions, inflicted several enemy casualties, and captured 50 prisoners.

In a bizarre twist, one group in captivity, surrounded McCarthy and seized his revolver. However they then inexplicably patted the relieved man on the back, and allowed him to return safely to his comrades! Overall McCarthy's contribution to the allied cause rivalled the revered achievements of Albert Jacka, and after he secured 500 metres of enemy trenches.

The London press labelled Laurie McCarthy "the super VC", but he later endured problems in civilian life. McCarthy was retrenched during the Great Depression, before fortunately finding employment again with Sunshine Harvester.

He remained with this firm he until he retired from the work force in 1969. Sadly, a son born to him and wife Florence,was KIA at Bougainville in 1945.

Laurie McCarthy was born in York, Western Australia, and from the age of four he was raised in a Catholic orphanage. In 1926, he and his own small family relocated to Victoria. Laurie McCarthy died at Heidelberg Repatriation Hospital in 1975.

Sergeant Stanley Robert McDougall

Sergeant Stanley Robert McDougall (1889-1968): joined the 47th Battalion, which became involved in heavy war action at Dernancourt France, on 28th March, 1918.

During the heat of battle, Sergeant McDougall killed two of enemy crew who were manning a Lewis gun. He then turned the captured gun on Germans crossing a railway line, which stalled their plans to establish a new position.

After his first round of ammunition was finished, McDougall seized a bayonet and fresh supplies of bullets. He then killed four enemies, including an officer. More fatalities resulted from his continued Lewis gun attacks, and he also captured 33 prisoners.

The Tasmanian born Stan McDougall commenced working life as a blacksmith, but later became a forest inspector in the island state's north-east. His work during periods of dangerous bushfires was described as "outstanding", and he was aged 79 when he passed away in Adelaide.

Sergeant Lewis McGee (1888-1917): was a member of the 40th Battalion which became involved in conflict near Ypres in Belgium, on 4th October, 1917.

Sergeant Lewis McGee

Sergeant McGee rushed a German concrete pill box, while armed only with a revolver. He shot some of the enemy, and captured the remainder of the group, which enabled his platoon to advance safely.

McGee also reorganised the remnants of his own group, and remained foremost in action for the remainder of the advance.

The Tasmanian born Lewis McGee was unfortunately KIA eight days later at Passchendaele. In civilian life McGee had been a railway engine driver, and he was survived by a wife and daughter, when he died at the age of 28.

Lieutenant Rupert Vance Moon

Lieutenant Rupert Vance "Mick" Moon (1982-1986) was a 22 year old bank clerk, when he enlisted in the AIF. He became an officer, and served with distinction in the 58th Battalion at Bullecourt France, on 12th May, 1917.

Lieutenant Moon's platoon was set the task of neutralising a machine gun shelter between enemy trenches. Despite being wounded in the fray, Moon successfully completed the mission, before receiving yet another wound, when the enemy was forced from their trench.

Grenades were used to trap the Germans, but the unfortunate Moon sustained a third wound when he was shot in the jaw. The gritty Lieutenant ensured that the platoon's hard gained position was consolidated, before he retreated to safety.

"Mick" Moon was a Victorian, who was born in Bacchus Marsh. In 1977 the then 85 year old Moon followed the examples of Sir Roden Cutler and Ted Kenna, when he planted a tree in the VC garden at Fort Queenscliff on Victoria's Bellarine Peninsula. Mick Moon later died in Geelong at age of 94.

Captain Henry "Harry" William Murray (1884-1966): saw action with the 13th Battalion, which became locked in combat near Gueudecourt, France on 4th May, 1917.

Captain Henry William Murray

Captain Murray was leading A Company, when they seized an enemy trench and consolidated their position. Three enemy charges were repelled, and the small group of 20 then drove the Germans from the area.

Murray carried the wounded to safety. He was a distinguished soldier, who was previously awarded a DCM at Gallipoli, and a DSO at Mouquet Farm on the Western Front

Harry Murray also served in World War 11. This highly decorated soldier began army life as a Private, and he finally became a Lieutenant Colonel. Murray was born in Tasmania, and purchased a grazing property at Muckadilla in Queensland, after World War 1 hostilities ceased.

Murray's first marriage was short lived, but he remarried after moving to New Zealand. His new bride and he then purchased another property near Richmond in Queensland. This shy, modest hero died of a heart attack following a car accident, near Miles in central Queensland. Harry Murray was 82 years of age at the time of his death.

Captain James
Ernest Newland

Captain James Ernest Newland (1881-1949): was born in the Geelong suburb of Highton, and he became a Tasmanian police officer before enlisting in the AIF. Newland was assigned to the 12th Battalion, which became involved in protracted action at Bourses and Lagnicourt in France on 7th, 9th and 15th April, 1917.

The allied group suffered many casualties during their initial advance near Bourses. However Captain Newland then led the group on a successful bombing raid of a ruined mill outside the village.

At 10pm on the same day, the Germans launched a vicious counter attack, but the extreme bravery and skill displayed by Newland helped stave off at least four spirited enemy assaults. Fortunately the 9th Battalion arrived on 12th April, and the combined forces were able to launch a victorious counter attack.

James Newland was born in Geelong, and he became a career soldier who rose to the rank of Lieutenant-Colonel, before retiring from the army in 1941. Eight years later, at the age of 68, James Newland died after suffering a heart attack in Melbourne.

Private Martin
O'Meara

Private Martin O'Meara (1885-1935): The Irish born private was assigned to the 16th Battalion, which saw fierce action at Pozieres France between 9th and 12th August, 1916.

Private O'Meara was a stretcher bearer, and he managed to rescue numerous wounded soldiers from "no man's land" during four days of heavy fighting.

He also provided precious supplies of food, water, ammunition and bombs to the trenches under siege.

After the war ended, a severely wounded Martin O'Meara spent most of his life in a mental hospital. He was aged 50 when he died in Perth.

Lance-Corporal Walter Peeler (1887-1968): was a member of the 3rd Pioneer Battalion, which became involved in fierce conflict at Broodseinde, near Ypres in Belgium, on 4th October, 1917.

Lance-Corporal Walter Peeler

Lance-Corporal Peeler was instrumental in pushing German snipers back into a shell hole, before accounting for nine of the enemy. This facilitated an advance from his unit, and Peeler repeated the action twice more, leading to further forays into enemy territory.

Peeler also located and killed a German machine gun operator, and overall the heroic Lance-Corporal accounted for 30 enemy soldiers.

After returning to civilian life, Wally Peeler worked as a Custodian at the Shrine of Remembrance in Melbourne. He passed away at the age of 81.

Lieutenant Charles Pope (1883-1917): An officer who served with the 11th Battalion, which saw action at Louverval in France, on 15th April, 1917.

Lieutenant Pope was placed in command of three posts at the centre of the Australian line. The entire group was killed by a large enemy force, and the Germans also lost approximately 80 soldiers in the fierce battle.

Charles Pope was born in London, and he relocated to Australia seven years before his death. Pope was a 34 year old married man, when he was KIA.

Lieutenant
Charles Pope

Sergeant William "Rusty" Ruthven (1893-1970): was a member of the 22nd Battalion, which was involved in a battle at Ville-Sur-Anere in France on 19th May, 1918.

When his battalion advanced, they suffered significant casualties. Sergeant Ruthven's commanding officer was included in the list of seriously wounded, whereupon Ruthven assumed command. He immediately made an impact, bombing the enemy post, and seizing a gun from a German he had bayoneted.

With this weapon, he then wounded two more of the enemy, and captured six others. Armed only with his revolver, Lieutenant

Sergeant William
"Rusty" Ruthven

Ruthven attacked another enemy group, killing a further two and forcing 32 others to surrender. For the remainder of the day, Ruthven appeared to be oblivious to heavy artillery fire around him, as he encouraged his men, and helped consolidate their position.

Bill "Rusty" Ruthven was born in the Melbourne suburb of Collingwood. He trained to be a mechanical engineer, and later served as a state Labour politician for 16 years. Bill Ruthven died in Melbourne, at the age of 77.

Private Edward John Ryan (1890-1941): was a soldier assigned to the 55th Battalion, which experienced dangerous action near Bellicourt in France, on 30th September, 1918.

Private Edward John Ryan

When his battalion attacked a German post, Private Ryan was among the first to reach their defences. Ryan's fearless endeavours inspired his comrades to overcome the enemy garrison, and, when the Germans launched a counter attack, he again featured prominently in the battle.

The 28 year old from Tumut in NSW led a group in a bomb and bayonet charge, killing three and forcing many others Germans into "no man's land". Ryan received a shoulder wound in this skirmish. However his actions enabled his comrades to capture the trench, and help Ryan clear the remainder of the enemy.

Sadly John Ryan did not adapt well on his return to civilian life. "Smiling Johnny" became a heavy drinker, who occasionally worked in labouring jobs as he drifted around various parts of the country. The thin, lithe little man died in Melbourne at the age of 51, and he was buried with full military honours at Springvale Crematorium.

Lieutenant Clifford William King Sadleir (1892-1964): was an officer with the 51st Battalion, which saw active service at Villers Bretonneau on 24th and 25th April, 1918.

Despite receiving a thigh wound, Lieutenant Sadlier accompanied Sergeant C.A. Stokes in a successful bombing attack, which netted the pair two guns and several enemy casualties.

Sadlier was wounded once more, when he attacked another German post, but he still managed to kill four more enemy soldiers. He then sustained yet another wound, but took control of their machine gun.

Cliff Sadlier was invalided from active service in 1918. He settled in Busselton, Western Australia, (WA), and became State Secretary of the Returned Soldiers League, (RSL). In 1936 he married Alice Smart, and he finished working life as a clerk in the Repatriation Department in Perth,

Sadlier was aged 72 when he died in

Lieutenant Clifford William King Sadleir

Busselton in 1964.

Sergeant Percy Clyde Statton (1890-1959)
was attached to the 40th Battalion, which
saw fierce action at Proyart in France on 12th
August, 1918.

Sergeant Percy
Clyde Statton

Sergeant Statton witnessed a failed 37th
Battalion attack. He and three comrades
reacted to this setback, by creeping to within
75 metres of the enemy strongpoint.

A revolver was Statton's only weapon, but he
led his group into the enemy trenches, seizing
guns and disposing of German troops. The
guns they captured were used to bring down
two other enemy crews.

After returning to the 37th Battalion,
Sergeant Statton became involved in battle
again, and during this action he rescued a
wounded commander, and recovered the body
of another comrade.

Percy Statton was born in the Tasmanian
town of Beaconsfield. After returning as a war
hero, he worked as a farmer and timber worker.
During the 1934 bushfires in the island state,
Percy Statton featured prominently in rescue
operations.

Statton married three times. His first wife
divorced him because he volunteered for
war service, and his second wife died. Percy
Statton lived until the age of 69, before he

died in Hobart, after losing his battle with stomach cancer.

Lieutenant Percy Valentine Storkey

Lieutenant Percy Valentine Storkey (1891-1969): The New Zealand born Storkey was a University student, when he enlisted in the AIF in 1915. Three years later the twice wounded Storkey had become a much respected platoon commander.

On the Western Front, Lieutenant Storkey was an officer with the 19th Battalion, which came under fierce fire at Hangard Wood in France, on 7th April, 1914.

The advance of Lieutenant Storkey's group was thwarted by approximately 80 heavily armed Germans. Storkey, and a group of 12 comrades, successfully charged the enemy post, capturing three officers and killing or wounding 30-50 of the enemy.

After the war ended, Percy Storkey completed his studies and joined a law practice. He later became a judge. Storkey was aged 78, when he died in England.

Lieutenant Edgar Thomas Towner (1890-1972): served as an officer with the 2nd Machine Gun Battalion, which was involved in action at Mont St Quentin near Peronne in France, on 1st September, 1918.

Lieutenant Edgar Thomas Towner

When the advance of his group was halted,

100

Lieutenant Towner singlehandedly captured a machine gun. With this acquired weapon, and their own Vickers machine guns, Towner and his men inflicted heavy losses on the enemy, and forced another 25 to surrender.

Towner then captured another machine gun, and, despite being wounded, forced the enemy to retreat. Thirty hours passed before Towner's injuries received medical attention, and, during his long wait, he continued to fight the enemy, until the medics arrived.

Edgar Towner was born in the Queensland outback near Blackall. He became a pastoralist, and remained a bachelor all his life. Towner died in Longreach at the age of 82.

Major Blair Anderson Wark (1894-1941): was Commander of the 32nd Battalion, which was involved in active service at both Bellicourt and Joncourt in France, between 29th September and 1st October, 1918.

Major Blair Anderson Wark

Major Wark deployed a nearby tank to deal with two enemy machine gun posts, before incorporating 200 leaderless American soldiers into his own ranks. During an advance, the group forced 40 enemy troopers to surrender. Four machine guns were also confiscated, along with ten German gunners, as Wark continued to lead the successful advance from the front.

The battalion inflicted heavy casualties

on the enemy, as they continued to acquire more machine guns, until the Beaurevoir Line was reached.

Blair Wark became the recipient of a VC for his brave actions at Bellicourt and Joncourt. Previously, at Polygon Wood in 1917, Major Wark had been honoured with a DSO, for displaying noteworthy valour in a combat situation.

Blair Wark was born in Bathurst NSW. He worked mostly as a quantity surveyor in civilian life, and, between the two world wars, he also served as a director in several companies. Wark re-enlisted in the AIF when World War 11 broke out, and during this conflict he was promoted to the rank of Lieutenant Colonel.

Unfortunately, at the age of 46, Blair Wark unexpectedly died after battling a short term coronary disease.

Temporary Colonel Lawrence Weathers

Temporary Colonel Lawrence Weathers (1890-1918): A New Zealand born officer with the 43rd Battalion, who became involved in fierce action at Peronne, France on 2nd September, 1918.

Despite enduring heavy fire, Temporary Colonel Weathers killed an enemy leader, when he rushed a garrison. Then, while being covered by Lewis gun fire, Weathers ran along a parapet, and dropped bombs into a German trench.

In this successful mission, 180 prisoners were taken and three machine guns confiscated.

Unfortunately, within a matter of months, Laurie Weathers was KIA. He was 28 years old when he died.

Sergeant John Woods Whittle (1883-1946): was a member of the 12th Battalion, which became involved in dangerous French conflicts at both Bourses and Lagnicourt, on 8th and 15th April, 1917.

Sergeant John Woods Whittle

After being involved in a successful bomb assault on an enemy position in a ruined mill, Sergeant Whittle was placed in a command situation. In this role, he reorganised his group, and attacked enemy troops who had launched a fierce counter attack.

Whittle, with the assistance of fellow VC recipient, Captain Newland, restabilised the Allies' position. The pair killed a German machine crew, and carried the captured gun back to their men. At the conclusion of the engagement, all allied positions in the area had been regained.

John Whittle was Tasmanian born, and prior to World War 1 he served in the second Boer War. He then enlisted in the RAN, where he was a stoker for five years. During the Great War, John Whittle became both a hero and a headache to military authorities.

In 1917 Sergeant Whittle was twice decorated, receiving a VC for the action described above, and a DCM for displaying conspicuous gallantry in conflicts at Le Barque and Ligny-Thillow. The three times wounded Whittle was always at the centre of any action, and at times he was a trouble magnet. During the war years, the incorrigible John Whittle faced court martial proceedings twice, on charges of unruly behaviour.

When World War 1 hostilities ceased, Whittle, his wife and growing family resided briefly in Tasmania, before moving to Sydney. In the harbour city John Whittle worked in the insurance industry, and later in a brewery. During his post-war life, Whittle again attracted headlines, after he recued and successfully resuscitated a drowning boy.

Whittle became the father of three girls and two boys. One of his sons, Ivan, lost his life at Port Moresby during World War 11, and Whittle himself died in Sydney at the age of 63, after suffering a cerebral haemorrhage.

Private James
Park Woods

Private James Park Woods (1891-1963): was a soldier attached to the 48th Battalion, which became engaged in a conflict at Le Verguier near St Quentin, France, on 18th September, 1918.

Private Woods was with a small party of Allied soldiers which attacked a well fortified enemy post. After Woods killed one German, approximately 30 others fled, leaving four heavy and two light machine guns behind them.

The acquired weapons were used to hold off determined enemy assaults. Woods played a pivotal role in the resistance, by throwing a succession of bombs into the enemy ranks, from the parapet where he was stationed.

After Jimmy Woods returned to civilian life, he took on the responsibility of raising his step sister. He was plagued by ill health for many years, and the Gawler born Jimmy Woods finally died in Perth at the age of 72.

**

OTHER WORLD WAR 1 VC WINNERS.

Temporary Lieutenant William Thomas Dartnell (alias Wilbur Taylor Dartnell), (1885-1915): was a serving officer with 25th Battalion, (Frontiersmen), the Royal Fusiliers, (City of London Regiment), which experienced war action at Makati, British East Africa, (now Kenya), on 3rd September, 1915.

Temporary Lieutenant William Thomas Dartnell

William Dartnell was Melbourne born, and when his schooling ended he became an actor. In 1901 a 15 year old Dartnell enlisted for service in the Boer War. After returning to Melbourne, William married. However he soon he returned to South Africa with his wife, and later enlisted for military service there, in World War 1.

Dartnell was assigned to the British based 25th Battalion, which became engaged in fierce action at Makati in present day Kenya. Despite being wounded during an ambush, Temporary Lieutenant Dartnell insisted in remaining with his group to assist more seriously injured mates. On two occasions he refused requests to leave, and actually asked his men to abandon him. Dartnell accounted for seven German soldiers, before he was KIA. This adventurous young man was dead at the age of 30.

Lieutenant Frank Hubert McNamara

Lieutenant Frank Hubert McNamara (1894-1961): was an officer with Unit 1 Squadron Australian Flying Corps, which was involved in a raid on Tel el Hesi in Palestine, on 20th March, 1917. Frank McNamara became the first Australian aviator to be awarded a VC.

That March day in 1917 became full of drama, after Captain David Rutherford, a pilot in the same flying corps, was forced to land his damaged plane behind enemy lines. Lieutenant McNamara, though seriously wounded in the same mission, came to Rutherford's rescue, after he saw a Turkish cavalry group galloping towards his stranded and injured mate.

On landing, the incapacitated McNamara

could not control his plane, and it turned over in a gully. After McNamara dragged himself from the wreckage, Rutherford managed to re-start his own plane, while McNamara kept the Turks at bay with his revolver. Fortunately, with assistance from two other pilots, the enemy advance was halted. The injured aviators became air borne, and flew the short 70 mile journey to safety. The self-effacing McNamara played down his role in the extraordinary escape, and modestly claimed he was only **"An ordinary man, thrust into the limelight by one truly amazing episode."**

Frank McNamara almost died while recuperating in hospital, after suffering an allergic reaction to a tetanus injection. He later married Helen Bluntschi, a Belgian woman he had previously met in war-time Cairo. McNamara then served in national aviation occupations, both in England and Australia.

He finally became Acting Air Vice –Marshall of the RAF. By then Frank McNamara was an embittered man, after being made redundant by the RAAF. He settled permanently in England, and insisted that his VC remain in London's RAF Museum, instead of being returned to Australia.

Despite his resentments, Frank McNamara is still remembered as being a quiet, scholarly and popular man. The 67 year old hero left a widow and two children after he died of heart failure, following a fall at his Buckingham home.

Sergeant Samuel George Pearse (1893-1919): was a Welsh born soldier, who served with the 45th Battalion Royal Fusiliers, Sadlier- Jackson's Brigade. This group became involved in significant action near Emstra in northern Russia, on 29th August, 1919.

Sergeant Samuel
George Pearse

Despite facing heavy artillery fire in his area, Sergeant Pearse cut his way through a barbed wire barrier, which cleared a path for his troops to enter. Pearse then singlehandedly bombed an enemy block house, and killed the occupants.

Unfortunately Pearse himself was cut down by machine gun fire during the fierce encounter, and he died in action at the age of 26.

Corporal Arthur Percy Sullivan (1896-1937): was also attached to the 45th Battalion Royal Fusiliers, Sadlier-Jackson's Brigade. Sullivan's heroism was especially noted, during an engagement at Dvina River near Archangel, north Russia, on 10th August, 1919.

Corporal Arthur
Percy Sullivan

Three regular soldiers and an enlisted officer fell into a swamp during a dangerous encounter. Despite coping with intense artillery fire, Corporal Sullivan jumped into the water on four separate occasions, and successfully rescued all his comrades.

In civilian life Arthur Sullivan was a shy man, who worked as a bank officer. He was born in the South Australian town of Crystal Brook, and died at the young age of 41.

CHAPTER SEVEN

WHEN WILL THEY EVER LEARN?

"Where have all the soldiers gone
Long time passing.
Where have all the soldiers gone?
Long time ago.
Where have all the soldiers gone?
Gone to grave yards everyone,
When will they ever learn?
When will we ever learn?"

Pete Seeger

During the early 1960s, Pete Seeger and Joe Hickerson confronted world leaders with searching questions, when they composed the protest song, "Where Have All the Flowers Gone?" The above timeless question, (when will they ever learn?), could well have been posed to the politicians and zealots who orchestrated the beginning of another massive global conflict in 1939. Tragically, this catastrophic war commenced a little over two decades after the worst recorded war in history.

Adolf Hitler

During the 21 year span between World War 1 and World War 11, the fortunes of Germany altered dramatically. Initially the harsh penalties imposed by the Treaty of Versailles, along with a collapsed economy, produced hard times for their people. Then, once economic conditions improved noticeably under a new leader named Adolf Hitler, the German's national pride was suddenly restored. Hitler's cruel targeting of Jews and other minority groups became conveniently overlooked by many, and the majority of Germans supported the expansionist policies, which their charismatic but highly dangerous leader initiated.

Western leaders of neighbouring countries observed Germany's growing aggression with disquiet. However, after the new Fuhrer ordered his troops to invade Poland, all appeasement attempts by other European leaders ended.

On 3rd September 1939, Britain declared war on Germany, and the Australian Prime Minister, Robert Menzies, quickly pledged our government's support for "the mother country". Supplies and foodstuffs were forwarded to Britain, and the production of war equipment was accelerated. The Australian -born Lieutenant- General Sir Thomas Blamey, was appointed commander of the 6th Division, which was available to serve either at home

Sir Robert Menzies

or abroad. By the end of 1939, this Division was stationed in Palestine. Then, when Italy became Germany's ally in June 1940, and French resistance began to crumble, training schedules took on a new urgency.

Australian volunteer forces were mainly sent to the Middle East, and between September 1940 and June 1941, they resisted German and Italian attacks on the north coast of Africa.

General Erwin Rommel

During April of 1941, other Diggers tried vainly to halt the German advance into Greece. Blamey believed that Menzies should not have allowed the British Prime Minister, Winston Churchill, to deploy some of our Middle East units there, as it weakened the defence of the Suez Canal and nearby oil fields. The diminished Australian presence in North Africa, resulted in General Erwin Rommel meeting little opposition, when he landed his German reinforcement at the Libyan port city of Tripoli.

However by New Year 1941, Allied forces made important advancements in their quest to defeat the Germans in North Africa. Numerous Italian strongholds were decimated, and the many weapons they abandoned appreciatively increased our arsenal of weapons. By January 1941, The Australian 6th Division was able to occupy the strategically important port settlement of Tobruk. Rommel, an inspirational

Sir Winston
Churchill

leader and master tactician, aimed to recover this loss, and annex all other Allied held areas in Libya. He then planned to occupy northern Egypt, and seize the Suez Canal.

Tobruk was an essential acquisition in this mission. The harbour was an ideal launching site for future transport of weapons to the Nile Valley and the Suez region. Soon the area between Tripoli and Tobruk became known as "Messerschmitt alley", after German war planes commenced their vicious bombing attacks.

Bengasi and El Regima were both seized by the powerful German war machine, and a resolute Winston Churchill implored the Australian Ninth Division to **"Hold Tobruk to the death".**

Churchill's message sounded ominously like "mission impossible", as the allies only had 30 tanks to defend the area, while Rommel had 300 at his disposal. General Sir Leslie James Morshead, the Australian commander of Allied forces in the area, could only maximise the limited resources he had. The stern taskmaster issued a defiant message to his troops, when he prepared them for a long siege.

"There will be no Dunkirk here. If we should have to go out, we shall fight our way out. There is no surrender, no retreat"

Ultimately, the 242 day siege of Tobruk

became the crowning achievement of Sir Leslie Morshead's military career. The former Ballarat teacher was 50 years of age, before he was promoted to command the 18th Brigade, and he then spent six months honing his men's fighting skills. In December 1939, he took his soldiers to the Middle East, and 16 months later he was made responsible for the defence of Tobruk.

Sir Leslie James Morshead

Australian war correspondent, Chester Wilmot, made the following assessment about Morshead's leadership capabilities.

"(He is) no military theorist: he is a hard, practical commander. A stickler for accuracy, he gives close attention to detail.. He is not a man of swift, bold or spectacular decisions, but once he has made up his mind on the right course of action, he sticks to it."

This stickler for detail was nicknamed "Ming the Merciless" by the rats of Tobruk, a title which indicate that the "King Rat" was not regarded with great affection by his men, even though he did gain their grudging admiration and respect.

After delivering his "Dunkirk" ultimatum, Morshead stepped up defence preparations. Concrete bunkers left by the Italians proved a useful acquisition, as they were a reasonably safe haven from air attacks, and would hold 14 soldiers when required. Overall, Morshead only had 14,000 Australian and 10,000 British soldiers to defend Tobruk, and the allies were vastly outnumbered by the enemy.

General Morshead decided to deploy lines of troops around the perimeter of the town. The outer defence was 15 kilometres from Tobruk, and was tagged the Red Line. Soldiers there formed a semi-circle to defend an area of approximately 45 kilometres. More trenches were dug, barbed wire restored and booby traps set around the pits. Initially results were encouraging for the Allies.

The Germans had no knowledge of the Red Line defence, and fared badly in "The Easter battle", a ferocious four day engagement, which began on Good Friday. Against all odds, the Aussie defence prevailed.

In one key battle, a team of five determined Diggers successfully defended an important stronghold against 30 Germans. After this crucial victory, Corporal J. H. Edmondson received a posthumous VC, for killing at least five enemy troops with his bayonet.

By Easter Monday, another German assault was imminent, and Morshead instructed his marksmen to hold their fire until the enemy advanced beyond the outer defence perimeter. The Germans appeared confused by these unconventional tactics, and suffered a huge casualty rate.

Morshead then added more minefields near the Red and Blue lines. He positioned them near the "25 pounders", field guns which were extremely effective at close range. Behind them was the mobile reserve. British and Aussie soldiers became used to the routine of grabbing some sleep during the day, and digging trenches and patrolling at night.

In April a better prepared Rommel launched a major air, sea and land operation, but the allies managed to thwart the assaults to some extent. Camouflaged fake gun positions were set up for attacks from the air, and the number of daytime ships in the Tobruk harbour area was reduced. On land, a fierce battle began for control of the Hill 209 garrison.

Initially, the Germans advanced well into the Allies' defence perimeter, and inflicted heavy losses. The 2/24th Battalion were decimated, the A, C and D company posts were overrun, and three company commanders were captured. By 4th May 1941, Hill 209 was in enemy hands. Rommel was then convinced that Tobruk would also fall into German hands.

However his ambitions were once more stalled by clever tactics. British artillery fire allowed the Allies to still wage battle on Hill 209, and counter attacks in the second week of May by the 2/13th Battalion, regained 320 metres of valuable territory. Rommel was forced to deploy over 30% of his declining number of troops to defend Hill 209, and his problems continued to grow.

German tanks were of little use in the heavily mined area, and their air strikes hit few significant targets. Also German tracer bullets were phosphorous tipped, so night attack positions were easily spotted by the allied forces. Furthermore, the Germans proved to be less skilled in close combat engagements.

Around that time, William Joyce, a Fascist radio broadcaster, dismissed the capabilities of General Morshead, describing him as the "Ali Baba" of the allied forces. His German propaganda broadcasts also inadvertently provided the Tobruk Diggers with a nickname which became famous. Joyce, whom the Aussies dubbed "Lord Haw Haw", because of his upper class English accent, referred contemptuously on air to "the rats (Diggers) running around in their trenches". Joyce's words immediately spawned a treasured nickname, and the "Rats of Tobruk" became famous for their resolute defence.

Rats of Tobruk

By then, a weird spirit of camaraderie had developed between the opposing forces. The combatants would ding each other on tin mugs, if they wanted to take a half-hour meal break from hostilities, and Australian and German soldiers would leave cigarettes for each other in "no man's land" areas. Rommel acknowledged the Australians "remarkable tenacity", and he ignored orders from Hitler to execute enemy commanders, who had become POWs.

Living conditions in the Tobruk trenches were uncomfortable and very basic. Hot bully beef was the standard meal for diggers, and the empty tins would then be used as toilets. Dysentery became rife, constant dust storms were unpleasant, temperatures soared to well over 40 degrees Celsius, and supplies of water were limited. Dust centipedes proved to be a constant nuisance, and the many wounded comrades present, added to the depressing scene. Hugh Barton Paterson, (the son of the famous poet, "Banjo"), expressed the beliefs of many "Rat" mates, with his poem "The Place They Call Tobruk"

> **"There's places that I've been in,**
> **I didn't like too well.**
> **New England's far too bloody cold,**
> **And Winton's hot as hell.**
> **The Walgett beer is always warm;**
> **In each there's something crook.**
> **But each and all are perfect,**
> **To this place they call Tobruk."**

General Morshead kept his troops hard at work, partly to counteract depression affecting the group. Later, when the 2/13th Battalion was granted well earned "R and R leave", after three months of front-line duties, Morshead encouraged them to relax and enjoy swimming activities in the nearby harbour.

By then diggers' thoughts had centred on the Pacific area, and the worrying news that Japanese aggression was posing threats to Australia. Their deployment from North Africa, however, was vigorously opposed by Churchill. Hundreds of

Australian lives would have been spared, if withdrawal had occurred then.

Morale declined after Morshead was transferred, and Major-General Scobie assumed command of the 2/13th Battalion. Withdrawal from Tobruk, which the "Rats" had clung to tenaciously for eight gruelling months, became a viable option. However, many heart breaking delays frustrated the exhausted soldiers. In October their rescue ship "Latona" was sunk, which cancelled out departure attempts for another month.

Rats of Tobruk

By then war in the Pacific had begun, but Churchill regarded the conflict there as being of secondary importance, compared to the battlefronts of Europe and North Africa. The battle fatigued "Rats" of the 2/13th were again urged to complete another "mission impossible".

"El Duda must be held at all costs," ordered the British Prime Minister.

Churchill's strong directive was hardly reasonable, as it pitted 160 "Rats of Tobruk" against at least 950 Germans. Another huge loss of life resulted, and one of the fallen was the promising poet, Captain Hugh Paterson.

However, once more the "Rats" prevailed. The enemy fled from a fierce bayonet attack, and on 7th December Rommel withdrew his troops. Three days later Italian and German forces relinquished Hill 209, and the allies had miraculously prevailed in the eight-month siege. Their units had begun to withdraw in October, but one Battalion remained until the siege was lifted in December.

Disaster remained with the besieged "Rats", as wounded members of the now famous 2/13th Battalion had their hospital ship bombed by German planes. Less than 40% survived the cowardly attack

Erwin Rommel later described the volunteer Australian soldiers as being "extraordinarily tough fighters- an elite formation of British Empire troops". Nine days after Pearl Harbour was bombed, the Australian land forces withdrew from Tobruk, which later returned to German control.

CHAPTER EIGHT

WORLD WAR 11 VCs IN EUROPE AND NORTH AFRICA

There were eight Australian VC recipients from World War 11 conflicts in Europe and North Africa.

Their names, together with brief citations about their lives and battlefield achievements, are noted below in alphabetical order.

Lieutenant Sir Arthur Roden Cutler (VC, AK, KCMG, KCVO, CBE), (1916-2002): An officer with the 2/5th Field Regiment. During conflicts at Merdjayoun on 19th June, 1941, and Damour, (6th July, 1941), in Lebanon, his sustained courage was outstanding against the Vichy French.

After being halted by the enemy in Syria, Lieutenant Cutler assembled a small group of men, and established an outpost in a house. Despite being under intense fire, Cutler repaired damaged telephone wires, which enabled reinforcements to arrive and engage the enemy.

Lieutenant Sir
Arthur Roden
Cutler

The seemingly fearless Cutler and his men, succeeded in driving back a tank attack, but he received a serious leg wound during the fierce battle. Medical attention was unavailable, until he was rescued 26 hours later. By then the wound had become septic, and the leg was later amputated.

Before the war, Roden Cutler had worked for Texaco, and in after work hours, he gained an Economics degree at Sydney University.

In post war years Cutler went on to represent Australia in important diplomatic roles. He served as High Commissioner in New Zealand. He was also the Australian ambassador in Pakistan, Ceylon, (now Sri Lanka), and the Netherlands. He once had a leadership role in a legation to Egypt. Overall, however, Sir Roden Cutler is best remembered for being NSW's longest serving State Governor, a role he fulfilled for the 16 years between 1966 and 1981.

Sir Roden's first wife died in 1990, after the couple had raised four sons. He re-married three years later, and was 86 years of age when he died in Sydney in 2002.

Corporal John Hurst
Edmondson

Corporal John "Jack" Hurst Edmondson (1914-1941): who served in the 17th Battalion, before being KIA at Tobruk in Libya, on 13th April, 1941.

In repulsing an enemy assault, Commander F.A. Macknell, Corporal Edmondson and five Privates, counter attacked with a spirited bayonet attack.

Though wounded in the neck and stomach, Edmondson bayoneted first one, and then another two Germans, who threatened the life of his commander. Another two Germans were KIA by Edmondson, but he died next morning at Post 33.

Jack Edmondson was born in the NSW town of Wagga Wagga, but moved with his family to Liverpool near Sydney, at an early age. He was a farm worker before he volunteered for military action and 27 years of age when he was KIA in North Africa.

Posthumously, Jack Edmondson became the first Australian soldier to be awarded a VC in World War 11. Today a commemorative clock honours his name in the Sydney suburb of Liverpool.

Acting Wing Commander Hughie Idwal Edwards (1914-1982): While serving with the No. 5 Squadron, RAF, Edwards performed with much valour in a bombing mission at Bremen, Germany, on 4th July, 1941.

In his Blenheim V6028 aeroplane, Acting Wing Commander Edwards led an important daylight bombing mission, on the heavily

Hughie Idwal
Edwards

defended German port of Bremen.

Four of the planes were shot down, as the squadron made a low level approach. However, after Edwards daringly led his team under high tension cables, no further losses were inflicted, and a successful bombing mission was accomplished.

Hughie Edwards was born in Fremantle, and he later served as State Governor of Western Australia between 1974 and 1975. He was aged 68 when he died in 1982.

Private James
Hannah Gordon

Private James "Jim" Hannah "Heather" Gordon (1909-1986): A soldier who served with the 2/31st Battalion, which saw fierce action at Jezzine, Lebanon, on 10th July, 1941.

Private Gordon's company came under severe threat, after an intense artillery attack killed three of its members, (including an officer), and wounded several others.

Gordon ignored the concerted fire and grenade attack, and wormed his way towards an enemy machine gun post, which had inflicted significant damage. Suddenly he then charged the post, and killed four machine gunners with his bayonet.

Jim Gordon's actions allowed his group to mount an attack which gained a gun post. After destroying their weapons and equipment, Gordon was again prominent in action, when his company fought their way back to the Battalion.

The following year, Jim Gordon became the model for a William Dargie painting which won the Archibald Prize. Previously Gordon had understated his age in order to enlist. When he "signed up" Jim Gordon unaccountably informed authorities that his middle name was "Heather"! He later served in New Guinea.

Civilian work was not to his liking, so Jim Gordon gladly became a career soldier. Later, after retiring from army life, he worked as a groundsman, before finally ending his workplace commitments.

Jim Gordon, a former resident of Gin Gin in Western Australia, was survived by his wife and son, when he died at the age of 77 in a Perth repatriation hospital.

Private Percival Eric Gratwick (1902-1942): was attached to the 2/48th Battalion, which fought a significant battle at El Alamein, Egypt, on 25th and 26th October, 1942.

Private Percival Eric Gratwick

His depleted group was forced to halt after enduring a concentrated attack which killed the platoon commander, a sergeant, and many others.

Only seven of the platoon was still alive, when Private Gratwick, armed with a rifle and bayonet in one hand, and grenades in the other, charged the nearest enemy post.

After hurling two grenades into the complex, Percy Gratwick killed the entire gun crew with his bayonet. He then charged another post, and inflicted more casualties, before being KIA by another machine gun, just metres away from an enemy trench.

Percy Gratwick was a native of Katanning in Western Australia, and worked as a prospector in the Pilbara region before enlisting. He was 40 years of age, when he died in battle.

Private Arthur Stanley Gurney

Private Arthur Stanley ("Stan") Gurney (1908-1942): was also a member of the 2/48th Battalion, which became involved in significant action at Tel el Elsa on 22nd July, 1942.

All officers in Private Gurney's unit were killed by machine gun fire during a fierce engagement. However, the gun post he invaded was silenced, after he bayoneted three enemy gunners. Two more enemy soldiers were taken out at the next post, and a prisoner taken.

Gurney was then knocked to the ground from the impact of exploding stick grenades, but he forged on to another gun post, where his dead body was later found.

Stan Gurney was born in the Western Australian settlement of Day Dawn, on the Murchison Goldfields. He was 33 years of age when he was KIA.

Sergeant William Henry ("Bill") Kibby (1903-1942): was another member of the 2/48th Battalion, which became involved in a conflict at El Alamein in Egypt, between 23rd and 31st October, 1942.

Sergeant William Henry Kibby

Sergeant Kibby was forced to assume command of his platoon, after the commander was KIA. After ordering his troops to attack an enemy machine gun post, Kibby fired his Tommy gun repeatedly at the enemy as he led the charge. Due to his brave actions, three Germans were killed, 12 taken prisoner, and the gun post was silenced.

Three days later the Germans launched fierce counter attacks, and Kibby maintained high morale in the platoon, while he mended broken communication links.

During the prolonged battle, Sergeant Kibby used grenades to destroy another enemy gun post, before he was KIA from machine gun fire.

Bill Kibby migrated from England to Adelaide with his family at the age of 11. Before the war began, he worked in a plaster works factory. Kibby was survived by a wife and two daughters, and this diminutive, out-door-loving man was aged 39, when he died at El Alamein.

Sergeant Rawdon
Hume Middleton

Flight Sergeant Rawdon "Ron" Hume Middleton (1916-1942): was a member of a RAAF Unit attached to the No. 149 Squadron, which participated in a vital bombing raid on Turin in Italy, between 28th and 29th November, 1942.

Flight Sergeant Middleton was involved in his 29th sortie, (one short of compulsorily ending his tour of duty), when he captained a Stirling BF372 on an air raid mission, which targeted the Fiat works in Turin.

After a dangerous journey over the Alps, Middleton made three low level altitude flights over the city to identify the key target. On the third exploratory trip, the windscreen of his aeroplane was shattered, and both pilots wounded, when the plane was struck by anti-aircraft fire.

Middleton's right eye was badly damaged by a shell splinter, and his jaw was shattered. The aircraft then suddenly dropped 250 metres, after the badly injured pilot lost consciousness. Fortunately the second pilot righted the plane, and the bombs were still released over their target.

After regaining consciousness, Flight-Sergeant Middleton ensured that his co-pilot received first aid, before guiding the damaged plane back towards England. The blood-covered Middleton experienced great pain, but he kept repeating the same determined intercom message to his crew:

"I'll make the English coast," he promised, "I'll get you home."

Only five minutes of fuel supplies remained, when the severely damaged plane crossed the English Channel, and Middleton ordered his men to parachute out of the plane.

Five of the crew obeyed his instructions and landed safely, but the flight engineer and front gunner stayed on board. They attempted to persuade Middleton to make a crash landing.

This would have necessitated landing in a residential area, and Middleton rejected that dangerous option. He turned back over the water, and the two remaining crew members parachuted into the Channel. Unfortunately they did not survive. Middleton's plane plunged into the sea after he ran out of fuel. His body was washed up on a beach near Dover a few days later.

Ron Middleton was born in Sydney, and he was a great nephew of the noted explorer, Hamilton Hume. He worked as a jackeroo on his father's NSW property, before joining the RAF.

The handsome and athletic young man was only 26 years of age when he was KIA.

CHAPTER NINE

THE PACIFIC CONFLICT

During the 1930s, Japan began to flex its territorial muscles. In that decade, tensions gradually increased between USA and Japan, after the latter country allegedly killed between 10,000 and 30,000 Chinese citizens in the 1937 Nanking Massacre. The relationship between the two countries deteriorated rapidly, when sanctions and embargoes imposed by America greatly reduced supplies of vital resources, to the highly populated Asian nation. Then, in 1940, Japan controversially formed a "mutual defence alliance" with Germany and Italy. This provocative agreement resulted in even more severe economic sanctions being imposed by the US government.

Simmering tensions between the two nations suddenly exploded into armed aggression on December 7th 1941. Early that day, Japan unexpectedly launched sustained aircraft bombing attacks on American military targets at Pearl Harbour in Hawaii. Two thousand three hundred American servicemen and civilians were killed, nearly 1,200 were injured, ten navy vessels were destroyed, and 188 aeroplanes were wrecked, during the devastating blitz.

Bombing of Pearl Harbour

Bombing of Darwin

Prime Minister
John Curtin

America and Britain immediately declared war on Japan, and a fearful Australian Government lobbied "the mother country" to have our British Empire troops quickly returned home, from the battlefields of Europe and North Africa.

The request was strongly opposed by Winston Churchill, who wanted our troops redeployed in Burma, so that India would be protected from any Japanese invasion. Churchill argued that any Pacific countries which fell to invading forces would be regained, once Germany was defeated in Europe and North Africa. In any case, declared the British war leader on Christmas Day 1941,

"Singapore will not fall."

Australia's wartime Prime Minister, John Curtin remained unconvinced, and he was understandably sceptical about Britain's commitment to our defence needs. Churchill's attempt to arbitrarily divert home-bound diggers to Burma was at odds with Australia's wishes, and Curtin's requests for a stronger British defence of Singapore were ignored. Consequently, on Boxing Day 1941, Curtin made an historic public announcement regarding Australia's future:

"Without any inhibitions...I make it quite clear that Australia looks to America, free from any pangs as to our traditional

links…with the United Kingdom.

Curtin then reminded the United States, about the mutual benefits which would flow from a proposed new alliance:

"Australia is the last bastion between the west coast of America and the Japanese. If Australia goes, the Americas are wide open."

Churchill was reportedly furious about Australia's dramatic dependency shift. However it was obvious that if an American military presence was not present in the region, Japan could more easily access its prime territorial targets. Its perceived "wish list" was Malaya (now Malaysia), the Dutch East Indies, (now Indonesia), and perhaps Australia. Before long, Curtin's foreign policy change was vindicated.

At the time, Singapore, "the Gibraltar of the far East", was our security blanket against the threat of foreign invasion. Since 1935, Britain had developed its strongest naval base there, and by the 1940s Singapore was regarded as being impregnable.

Misgivings were expressed when General Yamashita's 25th Army Battalion turned south towards the island fortress, after sweeping easily through Thailand and Malaya. Prime Minister Curtin, and Opposition leader, Menzies, both agreed that Britain's reaction towards these surprise land invasions was "totally inadequate". Criticisms continued after mid January 1942,

General Yamashita
Tomoyuki

Lieutenant-General
Arthur Percival

Lieutenant-General
Henry Gordon
Bennett

when Lieutenant-General Arthur Percival, the general officer commanding Malaya, ordered 30,000 British troops to retreat back to Singapore. However the Japanese were still outnumbered by an approximate ratio of 10:1, and it seemed unthinkable to suggest that Britain's heavily defended naval base would fall.

But by early 1942 key amenities, such as the island's reservoirs and pumping stations, were in Japanese hands. On February 15th of that year, (30 days ahead of Yamashita's schedule), an unthinkable possibility became a stark reality when Lieutenant-General Percival surrendered Singapore to Japan. By then Australia's commanding officer, Lieutenant-General Henry Gordon Bennett, had abandoned his leadership of the Eighth Division, and escaped from the island. Overall there is little doubt that the Japanese invaders were a well organised and more mobile group compared to the Allied troops, who were poorly led by both British and Australian commanders. It was Britain's worst defeat of World War 11, and Churchill reportedly never forgave Percival for surrendering the crucial Pacific defence base.

It is now more than 70 years since the fall of Singapore, but controversial claims still simmer about who was responsible for the debacle. British sources claim that approximately one third of Australian soldiers deserted their posts during the invasion, and a written report prepared by the British general Sir Archibald Wavell, declared that:

"For the fall of Singapore itself, the Australians are responsible."

During the early 1940s, the collapse of Singapore brought grave consequences to the Australian nation. A mammoth 15,000 Aussie servicemen became POWs, and public morale slumped across the shocked nation. It appeared then that the Japanese juggernaut was sweeping closer to our shores, and four days after Singapore surrendered, the grim situation appeared to worsen.

For the first time in our short history, Australia was attacked by a foreign nation. Approximately 200 Japanese fighter planes launched a massive assault on Darwin; the most comprehensive air attack since Pearl Harbour. At least 240 people were killed, and 400 wounded, in the savage 40 minute barrage, while 27 ships and 80 aeroplanes were severely damaged.

In early March, 1942, more "hits" were made on our northern settlements, with Broome, Townsville, Port Hedland, Katherine, Wyndham and Derby all being subjected to concentrated bombing attacks. By then Hong Kong, Malaya, Singapore and New Britain were all in Japanese hands, and the threat of full scale invasion for Australia appeared to be imminent. An aborted enemy submarine attack in Sydney harbour at the end of May increased growing paranoia across the country. The nation urgently needed its volunteer forces to be returned from abroad, and for America to play a decisive role in the Pacific conflict.

Thankfully an alliance with the United States was form-

General Douglas
MacArthur

General Sir
Thomas Blamey

alised, and the American General, Douglas MacArthur, was appointed as Supreme Commander of the South-West Pacific. Optimism increased after American naval forces gained significant victories in the Battle of the Coral Sea and at Midway, and these initial defeats for Japan, increased the pressure on their army campaign. Their goal of annexing New Guinea's, (now Papua-New Guinea's) vital base of Port Moresby would now have to be achieved by land invasion. From his Brisbane headquarters, MacArthur ordered General Sir Thomas Blamey, the Australian Commander of Allied Land Forces, to secure New Guinea's Kokoda Trail, against a potential invasion.

Australia was then demonstrably ill-equipped to meet such a formidable challenge. Our regular troops were either locked up in Japanese POW camps, or about to depart from far off European and North African campaigns. The fate of Australia was squarely in the hands of the "chocolate soldiers".

"Chocolate soldiers" or "Chocos" were deliberately insulting slang terms, used by career soldiers from AIF units, to describe new army recruits in the Citizens Military Forces (CMF). The battle-hardened volunteer veterans from AIF units were sceptical about the capabilities of CMF soldiers, who were assigned to serve alongside them in the future New Guinea conflict. They contemptuously dismissed these recruits from civilian life, as being "Chocolate soldiers" or Chocos".

There are two possible interpretations about the meaning of this slang term, which is still used to describe members of CMF units. "Chocolate soldiers" could mean that they will melt like chocolate once they experience the heat of battle. On the other hand, it may mean that these ill-prepared, clumsy recruits would soon be covered in mud, once they became engaged in jungle combat.

There is no doubt that the "chocolate soldiers" were poorly prepared, hastily trained, few in number, and mostly ignorant the about the formidable challenges that lay ahead of them. However, until it was possible for AIF units to arrive in New Guinea, they were the only option available.

Months later, the "Chocolate Soldiers" halted the Japanese advance along the Kokoda Trail for four crucial days, before AIF reinforcements could come to the rescue. It was then that the "Chocos" finally earned respect they deserved, from comrades who had previously scorned them.

CHAPTER TEN

THE BATTLE FOR THE KOKODA TRAIL

Japan faced serious dilemmas, following their naval defeats in the Coral Sea and at Midway. One military option was to target industrial areas on the east coast of Australia. Alternatively, the Japanese could establish bases in New Guinea and the Solomon Islands, from where they could block off sea and air access between America and Australia. They chose the latter policy, and planned a land invasion along the 96 kilometre Kokoda Trail, in New Guinea's rugged Owen Stanley Ranges, before seizing Port Moresby.

The task was so momentous, that the Allied Command Centre initially dismissed the idea as being totally impractical.

"(It's) just a 'boong track,' that an entire battalion couldn't cross," asserted Major General Basil Morris, the commandant of Port Moresby's 8th Battalion.

Morris's blunt views received widespread support from his colleagues.

"Fighting in this, (the Owen Stanley Ranges terrain), would be like fighting in a fog. You wouldn't know if

you were killing anything," stated Lieutenant William Alec Palmer.

Today one can still understand expressions of disbelief, about the Japanese hierarchy plans, to turn such a hostile environment into a war zone. The strategy involved climbing steep ridges in thick mist, where snakes, spiders and leeches were prevalent. Exposure to endemic tropical diseases such as malaria was always a threat. On average, 250 millimetres of rain fell nearly every day, and it was extremely humid by day, and freezing cold at night. Furthermore, the permanently wet conditions turned the trail into a mud heap for the weary soldiers, whose boots kept on sinking into the overused surface.

In his publication, "Green Armour", the Australian author and war correspondent, Osmar White, strongly summed up the challenging situation.

"Surely no war was ever fought under worse conditions than these. Surely no war has ever demanded more of a man in fortitude- even Gallipoli, Crete or the desert."

Both protagonists faced significant other problems in the New Guinea campaign. Japanese resources, due partly to the protracted struggle for Guadalcanal to the north of New Guinea, were being stretched to the limit. It was imperative for them to reach Port Moresby quickly, before food supplies and munitions ran out, and enemy reinforcements arrived.

The inexperienced Australians were vastly undermanned, they had fewer artillery weapons, supplies from the air were unreliable, and initially vital AIF support units were unavailable. Instead, experienced war veterans were undertaking jungle combat training in Queensland. Lieutenant-General Sydney Rowell, the Commander of 1 Corps, later described the

The Kokoda Trail

The Australian flag is raised over Kokoda

Lieutenant-General
Sydney Rowell

decision to hold back these soldiers from war action, as being "a cardinal error".

Remarks like this did not endear Rowell to his commanding officer, General Blamey. Rowell was later sacked by Blamey, and the removal of Rowell, and the also competent Brigadier Arnold Potts, was resented by the troops. Blamey, who inexplicably opposed camouflaged uniforms for our soldiers in the jungle terrain, frequently appeared to be out of touch with the whole conduct of the war. He was also quick to criticise young Diggers under his command. Fortunately, due to the diligence of war correspondent Chester Wilmot, and photographer Damien Parer, the Australian public were finally informed about both the Diggers' achievements, and the appalling conditions they endured

Blamey's disloyalty to his troops was graphically demonstrated on 9th November, 1942. On that day soldiers from the 21st, Brigade, and the decimated 2/14th, 2/16th and 2/17th Battalions, assembled at Owen's Corner, near the start or end of the Kokoda Trail. General Blamey was belatedly making his first visit to the New Guinea war zone from his Brisbane headquarters, and his public address shocked and infuriated the Diggers who were present.

The General ordered them to attack, to advance at all costs. He would tolerate no excuses, and stated that so far the campaign had been appalling.

"You have been defeated," Blamey shouted. "I have been defeated. Australia has been defeated...Always remember, It is the rabbit who runs who gets shot."

Observers later commented that Blamey was lucky to leave the gathering without being assaulted. No mention had been made, that the far from defeated Diggers, had successfully battled the odds of 6:1 in man-power. Furthermore, they opposed an enemy who cruelly tortured and executed many of their captured mates, and the Aussies were experiencing a high casualty rate.

The Diggers had virtually been described as being incompetent cowards, and reactions towards Blamey's insulting speech soon spread. When the General visited injured Aussie soldiers in a Port Moresby hospital, the angry patients munched lettuce leaves, and refused to speak to him. Later, Blamey was booed by 5,000 troops, when he appeared before them in an open- air theatre.

For most of the eight-month Kokoda offensive, the outnumbered Australians conducted a quick attack, followed by gradual retreat tactics. Ominously, crushing early defeats had forced them back up the track, but under the inspired leadership of Lieutenant-Colonel Ralph Honner from Western Australia, the Diggers thwarted the Japanese advance at Isurava.

Honner's mission there was to "hold the fort" until nearby reinforcements arrived. An estimated 464 soldiers from A, B, C and E Companies were at his command, and they were instructed to defend an area of 500 metres. Two emergency platoons were held back to fill any breeches in the defence.

The conflict at Isurava commenced on 26th August 1942, and for the next two days the embattled 39th Battalion appeared to be fighting a losing battle. Fortunately, when all appeared lost, platoon members of the 2/14th Battalion arrived, after trekking from Port Moresby. The Diggers then grittily defended Isurava for four crucial days. It was later estimated that the Japanese had a casualty rate of 10: 1 in that prolonged battle, which turned the tide of the campaign.

A jubilant Lieutenant-Colonel Honner later proudly proclaimed that:

"Isurava was not merely a battle on the Kokoda Trail, but Australia's Agincourt... There was... a burning desire to stick by (their) mates."

No-one embraced the spirit of mateship more at Isurava than Private Bruce Kingsbury, who was awarded a post humous VC, after inspiring his comrades with a brave but fatal Tommy- gun charge at the enemy.

Lieutenant Colonel
Ralph Honner

However invasion of Port Moresby by the Japanese still appeared to be a likely outcome. Only 150 Diggers from the original 464 remained to do battle, and at Isurava the huge casualty toll for the 2/14th Battalion was 48 dead, 44 missing and 150 wounded. By mid September the now starving Japanese troops could see the lights of Port Moresby. At

least 90% of their original mission had been accomplished, though large numbers of Allied reinforcements had increased the chances of a strong rearguard action.

Then an unexpected bonus was delivered to the Aussies. On 23rd September 1942, General Hori received orders, from the Japanese headquarters based in Rabaul, to "advance to the rear and consolidate at Buna". By that stage, Japan's recent loss of airways control at Milne Bay, the past setbacks of their navy at Midway and the Coral Sea, and the stalemate which still prevailed in the struggle for Guadalcanal, had finally drained their resources. On 26th September, the disappointed Japanese soldiers began to retreat down the Kokoda Trail. When Digger forces pursued the departing enemy, nauseating signs of cannibalism, became increasingly evident.

General Hori

The battle carnage continued, but when Buna finally fell to the Allies on 21st January, 1943, the war in New Guinea was drawing to a close. By March, the Americans and Australians had evicted Japanese out of Guadalcanal in the Solomon Islands, and 30 months later the war officially ended.

Two thousand one hundred and sixty-five Australian were KIA during the New Guinea campaign, and 3,533 were wounded. The United States lost 671 servicemen, while 2,172 were wounded. At least 13,000 of the Japanese forces were killed, and many more injured.

"Now on Kokoda Day. When all the names are read out of those killed in action, I still see them as they were. They will never become old or embittered. Just laughing kids forever." (A tribute from Kokoda veteran, Private Burton.)

General Hori's white horse was found drowned at sea, and it is presumed the flamboyant Japanese commander met the same fate. Colonel Honner was awarded a DSO and MC, but war wounds hospitalised him for ten months, and he was discharged from the army in 1945. In civilian life Ralph Honner served as an administrator on the War Pensions Assessment Tribunal, and between 1968 and 1972, he was Australia's Ambassador in Ireland. Honner was 89 years of age, when he died in 1994.

Soon after the war ended, Thomas Blamey lost his position as Commander of the Australian Army. Lieutenant-General Sir Vernon Sturdee briefly replaced him, and between 1950 and 1954, Blamey's old rival, Sydney Rowell, was appointed to the Army's most senior post.

Prime Minister John Curtin passed away in July 1944, and General MacArthur, (who had been frequently dismissive about Australia's role in the Pacific conflict), was generous in his praise.

"Mr. Curtin was one of the greatest of wartime statesmen. He was one of the greats of the Earth."

CHAPTER ELEVEN

KOKODA HEROES

Twelve Australian servicemen were awarded World War 11 VCs in the Pacific conflict.

Their names are listed below in alphabetical order, together with citation details which led to the prestigious medal being awarded. In some cases, brief biographical details are included.

Lieutenant-Colonel Charles Groves Wright Anderson (1897-1988): Anderson was appointed as Temporary Commander of the 2/19th Battalion, which became involved in dangerous action at Muar River in Malaya, between 18th and 22nd January, 1942.

During the Japanese land invasion of Malaya, Anderson assumed command of a brigade which had suffered heavy casualties. Previously the group was isolated and disorganised, but under Lieutenant-Colonel Anderson's leadership they became a potent force.

After two days of heavy fighting, the leading company

Lieutenant-Colonel
Charles Anderson

penetrated vital enemy resistance on a bridge, before Anderson, (accompanied by his group singing a spirited rendition of "Waltzing Matilda"), led a successful attack. The singing soldiers made two machine gun posts inoperable with grenade attacks, and Anderson shot and killed two Japanese gunners with his revolver.

Brigadier Duncan was unfortunately KIA, but Anderson effectively took control, and organised a three-company attack, which routed the enemy. Soon after, he commanded a large group in forays around the Parit Sulong area, where they again suffered severe casualties. Their artillery and mortar ammunition supplies were also quickly depleted.

Evacuation from the area became essential, a tactic which Lieutenant-Colonel Anderson planned with great skill. Vehicles and many guns were destroyed, rather than being left behind for the enemy, and his troops withdrew discreetly from danger, in small groups.

Charles Anderson was captured on 15th February 1942, and interned in a Japanese POW camp until 1945. He was born in Cape Town, and served in the military forces there, until his wife and he migrated to Australia when he was 34 years-of-age age.

Anderson became a farmer in the Riverina area of NSW, and his wife and he raised four children. In 1949 he was elected to Federal

Parliament, after he contested the seat of Hume for the Country Party. Anderson lost the seat in 1951, but regained Hume in 1955, and remained a parliamentarian until 1961. Charles Anderson then relocated to the Canberra suburb of Red Hill, and he was 91-years-of-age, when he died in the national capital in 1988.

Lieutenant Albert Chowne (1920-1945): was an officer with Unit 2/2nd Battalion, which became involved in intense action at Dagua in New Guinea on 25th March, 1945.

Lieutenant Albert Chowne

When making their way up a small rise, the group came under heavy fire from concealed machine guns. The platoon commander was included among the list of casualties.

Lieutenant Chowne rushed up the steep, narrow track, and threw grenades which "took out" two enemy machine gun posts. Though seriously wounded in the attack, Chowne killed two more Japanese before being KIA.

Albert Chowne was born in Sydney, and was 25 years of age when he died. He had then been married for a little over a year, and was previously employed as a shirt cutter with David Jones. Before being transferred to New Guinea, this self-effacing young man served with distinction in the North African campaign.

Sergeant Thomas
Currie Derrick

Sergeant Thomas Currie "Diver" Derrick (1914-1944): was assigned to Unit 2/48th Battalion, which became engaged with enemy forces at Sattleberg, New Guinea on 24th November, 1943.

Derrick's group was ordered to outflank a strong enemy position on a cliff face, before mounting an attack. However, attempts to scale the steep assent had to be aborted, due to heavy artillery fire from above.

After obtaining permission to individually mount another attack, Sergeant Derrick threw grenades into the gun post which had halted their advance. His continued grenade attacks on other enemy defence posts caused the demoralised Japanese soldiers to flee, leaving their own grenades and other weapons behind. Derrick's actions at last gave the 2/48th Battalion a foothold on the precipice.

Derrick returned to his group, which captured three more enemy defence posts. In total, he contributed to the silencing of ten such positions, but the 30-year-old Adelaide man was later KIA on 24th May at Tarakan Island in Borneo.

"Diver" Derrick married during the war, and he also served in the Middle East, where he was awarded a Military Medal. In civilian life, Derrick was an itinerant worker.

Corporal John "Jack" Alexander French (1914-1942): was attached to Unit 2/ 9th Battalion at Milne Bay, New Guinea, on 4th September, 1942.

Corporal French's battalion came under heavy fire while crossing a creek near Milne Bay. After ordering his group to take cover, French advanced alone and silenced a gun post with a hand grenade attack.

Corporal John
Alexander French

He returned briefly to his group to replenish his supply of grenades, and then made a second post inoperable. French used a Thompson sub-machine gun to kill 60-70 occupants of a third post, which ended the Japanese resistance. Unfortunately Corporal French was KIA during that assault on the enemy.

Jack French was born at Crow's Nest near Toowoomba, Queensland, and was an apprentice barber in civilian life. He was 28 years old when he died,

Private Richard Kelleher (1910-1963): was a soldier with the 2/25th Battalion, which experienced heavy war action near Nadzab, New Guinea, on 13th September, 1943.

Private Kelleher's platoon came under heavy fire from a machine gun post 50 metres away. In the attack, Commander "Billy" Richards and two others were wounded, and five others killed.

Private Richard
Kelleher

Kelleher announced he was going to rescue his commander. He rushed the nearby post, and hurled two grenades into the enemy camp. Private Kelleher then returned to the platoon and collected a Bren gun, which he used to silence the Japanese gun post. Kelleher then braved heavy enemy fire, and rescued his wounded section leader.

Richard Kelleher was born in County Kerry, Ireland, and migrated to Australia with his sister. Malaria affected his health after the war, and he worked as a gardener in Melbourne until he died at the age of 53. Kelleher was survived by his widow, who later remarried.

Private Edward Kenna

Private Edward "Ted" Kenna (1919-2009): was a member of the 2/4th Battalion, and he displayed conspicuous bravery at Wewak, New Guinea on 15th May, 1945.

After several members of his unit were wounded from heavy machine gun fire, Private Kenna, on his own volition, stood up in full view of the Japanese gun post 50 metres away. He then commenced firing at the enemy with his Bren gun.

During the gun battle, bullets appeared to pass between Kenna's arms and legs, but he continued firing from the hip, until the gun post was nullified. Many Japanese were killed by Kenna, and when his Bren gun magazine exhausted its supply of ammunition, he called for a rifle. The skilled marksman then shot down the opposing gunner with his first round of fire. A second machine gunner opened up, and Kenna shot him as well. No further injuries were inflicted on his own platoon, once Ted Kenna launched his own personal attack, and his incredible bravery ensured his company's success.

Two weeks later Kenna was shot in the mouth, when he attempted to repeat the previous Wewak effort, and he was hospitalised for nearly a year. Ted Kenna married after being discharged from the army in 1946. His bride was Marjorie Rushberry, who had nursed him during his recuperation at Heidelberg Military Hospital in Melbourne.

The couple raised four children, after returning to Ted's home town of Hamilton, where Ted worked for the shire council and played football with a local club. This "knock about" character became readily available to attend public functions Fellow guests of honour were often other surviving VC winners, such as Keith Payne, Mark Donaldson and Ben Roberts-Smith.

In his later years Ted Kenna, VC, became a resident of a nursing home in Drysdale. He was 90 years of age, when he passed away in Geelong in 2009.

Private Bruce Steel Kingsbury (1918-1942): A valiant soldier who served with 2/14th Battalion, which became engaged in a crucial battle at Isurava in New Guinea, on 29th August, 1942.

"This soldier, this warrior, was far braver than any in Japan. I think, and when I think about it now, it still affects me". (A tribute from Private Shiganori Doi, a

Private Bruce
Steel Kingsbury

former soldier with the 144th Japanese Regiment).

On the afternoon of 29th August, after his platoon had been largely decimated, Private Kingsbury volunteered for a counter attack on the enemy, who appeared likely at any time to breech the Diggers' defence.

Firing his Bren-gun from the hip, and screaming abuse as he charged, Bruce Kingsbury rushed down a hill, and cut a swathe through the astonished Japanese ranks. Kingsbury accounted for at least 30 enemy soldiers, and his mates who looked on, never forgot Kingsbury's instinctively brave charge, when enemy bullets almost appeared to bounce off him. Many of his comrades were inspired to follow his lead, and they added their own withering fire as they advanced.

Then, just when the courageous hero appeared to have survived, a lone Japanese sniper stood up and fired a single shot, while Kingsbury was reloading his Bren gun.

The gallant Aussie slumped to the ground, and Private Alan Avery, his best mate since schooldays, rushed Kingsbury back to the Regimental First Aid Camp. There Dr. Don Duffy gently informed Avery that Bruce Kingsbury had been killed, and the hero's friend was devastated.

"What do you say to a dying man" (tribute poem penned by Sergeant Bede Tongs, 3ʳᵈ Battalion).

> **"Just three minutes ago he was so full of life,**
> **Firing his Bren from his hip.**
> **When all of a sudden he's hit!**
> **..And my best mate falls**
> **Close to my feet.**
> **'Tell them I tried,' he said,**
> **And my words of good-bye**
> **Froze on my lips."**

Bruce Kingsbury was born in Melbourne. He qualified as a printer, but worked in a variety of jobs, as he roamed between Melbourne and Sydney, with Avery constantly by his side. Kingsbury's posthumous VC was the first to be awarded on Australian administrative territory. He was only aged 24 when he was KIA.

Sadly, ongoing grief marred the rest of Alan Avery's days. After returning to civilian life, he became a heavy drinker, and his marriage collapsed. With his health failing, the restless nurseryman attempted to turn his life around by moving to Queensland. However war memories continued to haunt him, and in May 1995, Alan Avery shot himself dead.

Corporal John "Jack" Bernard Mackey (1922-1945): was attached to the 2/3ʳᵈ Pioneer Battalion, which became involved in dangerous war action on Tarakan Island in Indonesia on 12ᵗʰ May, 1945.

Corporal Mackey's group was moving along a narrow path,

Corporal John
Bernard Mackey

when they became subjected to heavy fire near the top of a steep ridge. Mackey charged two machine gun posts, and overwhelmed enemy soldiers there in hand-to-hand struggles. He then used grenades to destroy the heaviest machine gun post.

Mackey then disposed of two more Japanese soldiers with an Owen gun, before he was shot dead by machine gun fire.

Jack Mackey was born in Sydney, and he served with distinction in North Africa, after enlisting in the AIF. He was 22 years of age when he was KIA.

Flight Lieutenant
William Newton

Flight Lieutenant William "Bill" Ellis Newton (1919-1943): was an officer with Unit 22/ 22 Squadron of the RAAF, which became involved in significant action over Salamua Isthmus, New Guinea, on 10th March, 1943.

It was two days before his final flight, when Flight Lieutenant Newton led a low level air attack, under heavy fire. Though his plane was repeatedly hit, Newton successfully bombed his target, destroying many enemy buildings and fuel storage units in the process. He then managed to land his damaged plane safely.

On returning to the fray, Newton targeted a single building, and scored a direct hit, before his own plane burst into flames after being struck by anti-aircraft fire. Somehow Newton saved his crew, when he crash landed in deep water, but he was captured by the Japanese.

Days later Bill Newton's headless body was discovered at Salamua.

Bill Newton was a handsome, flamboyant man who was described as having "the dash of an Errol Flynn or Keith Miller". The Melbourne born Newton excelled in a variety of sports, and he was 23 years-old when he was KIA. A memorial panel still honours his name in St. Kilda's old Presbyterian Church.

Private Frank John Partridge (1924-1964): was a soldier assigned to the 8th Battalion, which became involved in significant war action at New Guinea's Bonis Peninsula, on 24th July, 1945.

Private Frank John Partridge

Private Partridge received wounds to his left arm and thigh in a concerted attack from the Japanese. Despite continuing to be barraged by heavy fire, Partridge retrieved a Bren gun from a dead comrade. This weapon provided cover fire when Partridge overwhelmed a nearby enemy bunker with a grenade attack.

After killing one Japanese soldier with his knife, blood loss caused Partridge to abandon his takeover attempt of another bunker. His platoon was inspired by his heroic actions to also advance forward. The badly wounded Partridge soon returned to the action, before his platoon was again driven back.

When the war ended, Frank Partridge returned to the family farm near Macksville, NSW, where he had worked before enlisting in the army. The apparently confirmed bachelor lived with his father in a dirt floored farmhouse. At night he self- educated, reading volumes of "Encyclopaedia Britannica" by the light of a kerosene lantern,

Partridge discovered that he had a photographic memory, and he became a highly successful "Pick a Box" contestant on national television. Viewers warmed to Frank's laconic personality, in entertaining general knowledge duels with celebrities such as Barry Jones. The highly successful Frank Partridge became one of only three contestants, to pick all 40 of the contested boxes.

Partridge in a Pick A Box program

In today's terms, Frank Partridge won the equivalent of $A250,000 from his media venture, and in 1963, he unexpectedly married a 31 year old Sydney nurse. He also unsuccessfully attempted to gain Country Party pre-selection for the Federal seat of Cowper, during the same year.

Frank Partridge was unfortunately killed in a car accident a year later. He was survived by his widow and a three month old child, and was 39 years of age when he died.

Corporal Reginald Roy Rattey (1918-1986): was attached to the 25th Battalion, which became involved in a fierce battle near Buin road, South Bougainville, on 22nd March 1945.

Corporal Rattey repeatedly fired his Bren gun, when he acted alone in an attempted weapon pit takeover. He then used grenades to silence three enemy posts.

Corporal Reginald Roy Rattey

While under heavy fire, Rattey returned to base to collect more grenades, before killing or routing the crew from another post. Rattey's single handed and brave assaults resulted in success for his section within an hour.

At the conclusion of the war, Reg Rattey returned to West Wyalong where he became a soldier settler. His first marriage, from which a child was born, ended with his wife's death. After remarrying, his second wife and he raised another four children.

After ending his farming career, Reg Rattey captured tiger snakes for a Gosford Reptile Park, and he also worked as a commercial fisherman. He passed away at the age of 68. Reg Rattey was honoured with a full military funeral in his home town.

Private Leslie Thomas "Tom" Starcevich (1918-1989): was a soldier assigned to 2/43rd Battalion, which was ambushed by enemy

Private Leslie Thomas Starcevich

soldiers near Beaufort, British North Borneo, on 28th June, 1945.

Private Starcevich's group suffered significant casualties after they came under artillery attack, on a single track in a wooded spur. Using his Bren gun, Tom Starcevich killed five Japanese soldiers, scattered many more of the enemy, and silenced gun posts which had previously ambushed the Diggers. He later killed a further seven Japanese soldiers, in order to secure another gun post.

Tom Starcevich was born at Grass Patch near the Western Australian town of Esperance, and he was buried in the Esperance Cemetery. He died at the age of 71.

" THE 'FUZZY WUZZY' ANGELS."

"Slow and steady in bad places,
On the awful mountain track.
And the look upon their faces
Makes you think that Christ was black."
(Tribute poem by Sapper Bert Beros).

No VCs were awarded to indigenous stretcher bearers on the Kokoda, but the "Fuzzy Wuzzy' Angels" became war heroes to countless Diggers in the New Guinea highlands.

They nurtured the sick and injured Aussie soldiers uncomplainingly, and the courage and stamina displayed by these stoic people, was amazing.

Their success rate was also outstandingly high; allegedly, all but four of the wounded carried out on stretchers, failed to survive.

CHAPTER TWELVE

KOREA; THE FORGOTTEN WAR

It appears fashionable to label various conflicts as being "forgotten wars", but in the long battle for control of Korea, this assessment appears to be true. The current outcome, after approximately 75,000 people were killed on the Korean Peninsula in the 1950s, remains a political status quo; a capitalist south and the communist north, still control separate areas of the country. In 1950, the demarcation line between the two countries was the 38th parallel. This division remains the border line today.

World War 11 ended nearly five years before the conflict flared, and the Korean War was fought with new and more potent weapons. Jet powered fighter planes and helicopters made their debuts in the armed struggle.

Previously the United Nations (UN) had voted to hold elections which would give the majority party the right to govern the whole country, but North Korea refused to take part. This decision led to the Republic of South Korea being formed in August, 1949.

Less than a year later, on June 25th 1950, the Chinese styled Republic of North Korea, shocked the world when it sent armed troops across the border. An immediate UN Security Council meeting passed a motion, (sponsored by the USA), for North Korea to withdraw behind the 38th parallel. It was emphasised that refusal would result in UN peace forces restoring the boundaries, with armed intervention.

North Korea ignored the warning, and its forces experienced early success. In the first three days of the conflict, troops led by Kim il Sung seized Seoul, the capital of South Korea. It was the beginning of a blitzkrieg plan by North Korea, which aimed to deliver the whole Peninsula to communist forces, before the Western world had time to react effectively.

Australia was involved in the fray from the very start. Two days after America committed air and sea forces to the defence of South Korea, Prime Minister Menzies placed a frigate and a destroyer at the UN's disposal. A squadron of Japanese-based Australian Mustangs, was also placed on alert. In early July, General Douglas MacArthur was appointed Commander in Chief of the UN forces, and by July 26th, Australia, Britain and New Zealand all committed ground troops for war action on the Korean Peninsula.

MacArthur soon boldly took the initiative. His tactic of opening up a second line behind enemy supply bases, proved very effective, and by September 29th early North Korean gains had been totally reversed. The allies appeared poised to seize the communist's capital city of Pyongyang, an outcome which would basically end the war. However a serious error of judgement by the brash General MacArthur dramatically changed the conduct of the war.

China had previously warned that it would intervene if foreign troops ventured close to their borders. However MacArthur assured US President Harry Truman that the Chinese were bluffing. Furthermore, asserted the Commander in Chief, these "Chinese laundrymen" would quickly be slaughtered, if they entered the conflict.

However, the momentum of the conflict shifted decisively towards the communists, after UN forces pushed North Korean forces close to the forbidden border. A mammoth force of 300,000 Chinese soldiers suddenly entered the armed struggle, which resulted in UN troops being forced back. Casualty rates soared within peace keeping forces, and Seoul again fell into enemy hands. America was humiliated, after making its longest retreat in military history.

Truman sacked MacArthur, after accusing him of insubordination, and in later years the President provided candid comment about his dramatic decision.

"I fired him because he wouldn't respect the authority of the President. I didn't fire him because he was a dumb son of a bitch, although he was, but that's not against the law for Generals. If it was half, (even) three quarters of them, would be in jail."

Before Chinese General Peng Dehuai

President Harry Truman

Commander
Ben O'Dowd,

launched his 5th Offensive, Australian and Canadian soldiers began assisting the South Korean 6th Division in the defence of Kapyong Valley. Their combined role was to block strategic positions on the hills from enemy attacks. It later proved to be a challenging task, as Allied battle lines were far apart, and the number of Aussie troops involved was thinly spread.

Before long the valley was full of South Korean refugees, who were fleeing from around 10,000 advancing Chinese soldiers. Seven hundred Australians, and much the same number of Canadian troops, were asked to defend the area, and the night of April 23rd became a desperate time of survival. In between short lulls, the Chinese enemy blew whistles and bugles, as preludes to yet another mass attack.

"When the bugles and whistles stopped, we knew they were on their way," recalled Commander O'Dowd, just before 2011 Anzac Day ceremonies began. "Some of their soldiers did not carry weapons - just bucketfuls of grenades."

Much ground was lost by the defenders, and by next morning four Australian companies were forced to withdraw.

In the absence of Battalion Commander Bruce Ferguson, O'Dowd, who was the Senior Rifle Company Commander, took charge of the night retreat. Great care was taken to ensure the wounded from the Australian forward companies were carried out safely, and ultimately no lives were lost in the withdrawal. Historian Bob Breen later described Commander O'Dowd's performance as being "a superb military feat". Ben O'Dowd later fathered nine children and lived to the age of 93 before he died at his Mt. Waverly home on 29th February 2012. Surprisingly this fine soldier and community service volunteer was never mentioned in Korean War despatches.

American tank at Kapyong

Five hundred Chinese were killed on April 23rd at Kapyong, which is the highest enemy casualty rate ever claimed in a single day by a Commonwealth Unit. In comparison, the Australian toll, (32 killed, and 53 wounded), was relatively low.

The Diggers at Kapyong proved themselves worthy heirs of

Lieutenant-Colonel
Charles Green

the Anzac tradition. However after that fierce encounter, the war virtually became a trench dominated stalemate, before a ceasefire was declared in July 1953. No peace agreement was ever signed, and shelling attacks of South Korea from the North, still sporadically occur, nearly 60 years after the war officially ended.

Australia paid a high price for its involvement in the Korean War. Close to 300 were declared either dead or missing, and more than 1,200 were wounded. Total UN losses came to 73,500.

VC awards were overlooked for Australian service personnel in "the forgotten war". However the 3 Royal Australian Regiment, (RAR), proudly led by Charlie Green and Ben O'Dowd, received a Silver Star citation from the US government, for its outstanding performance at the battle of Kapyong. This was a prestigious compliment, as no further Silver Star awards were forthcoming for Australians, until the 6RAR received this honour, for their contributions at the Battle of Long Tan in Vietnam.

Lieutenant-Colonel Charles "Charlie" Hercules Green, remains a legend of the 3RAR Regiment. Previously, during the New Guinea conflict, a then 25 year old Charlie Green became the youngest leader of an Australian World War 11 group of soldiers, after he was appointed Commander of the 2/11 battalion, which mostly saw action in the Aitape-Wewak campaign.

In the Korean conflict, Green's reputation continued to grow. He was regarded as a natural leader-one who gained the affection and respect of his men, because of his concern for their welfare, and his coolness under pressure.

Charlie Green was KIA only a day the day after he led the 3RAR to an impressive victory at Chongju, where only nine Australian soldiers were lost in that October 1950 battle, while at least 150 North Koreans died in action. Unfortunately, Green's tragic demise was very much an unlucky example, of being in the wrong place at the wrong time.

He had not slept for 48 hours during the bitter hostilities at Chongju, and was slumbering under a tree when a lone enemy missile exploded exactly where he was bedded down. Despite suffering dreadful stomach wounds from shrapnel, General Green was still concerned about his units' safety and welfare, when he was being transported to the base medical centre. Unfortunately the brilliant soldier did not recover, and one of Australia's most promising military officers was dead at the age of 30.

Previously, after returning from World War 11 action, Charlie Green had married, and become the father of a daughter. Years later his widow, Olwyn, wrote his biography, titled "The name's still Charlie".

Battle of Kapyong scene

Kapyong daylight patrol

CHAPTER THIRTEEN

VIETNAM; THE CONTROVERSIAL WAR

Australian forces fought in Vietnam for the decade between 1962 and 1972. It remains our longest war commitment, and many lives were lost, and many lives were dramatically changed by the conflict. From the Allies' perspective, Vietnam also became a war that was never won.

Between the 1960s and early 1970s, the Vietnam War was a topic fiercely debated within Australian society. The issue finally split the nation, and caused serious social disruption, the likes of which had not been experienced, since the conscription referendums of World War 1. Many draft resisters, conscientious objectors and protestors, were either fined or jailed. Unfortunately, some serving soldiers received hostile receptions, after they arrived home from the battle front.

To a large degree, Australia's involvement in the Vietnam War was politically based; we were there to keep faith with the American alliance. Many citizens still believed that the involvement of US military forces saved our country from Japanese invasion in World War 11. Consequently, we were "ever ready" to support the USA, first in Korea, and later in Vietnam.

America's strong commitment to both conflicts, was largely motivated by the fear that communism could spread globally, and greatly endanger the capitalist way of life, which was favoured by Western nations.

The perceived problem became known as "the domino theory", a belief which originated from the successful 1949 communist uprising in China. In essence, the domino theory supported the view that if a nation, such as China, embraced communist rule, then neighbouring countries would fall like dominoes to aggressive anti-capitalist groups.

Previously, in the early 1930s, Australia had supported the French backed Viet Minh government in Vietnam, even though the government had been toppled by communist armed forces. Prime Minister Menzies reaffirmed this policy in 1957, and at the time, his stand received wide support from the Australian public.

Conscription issue in World War 1

Pledges were transferred to actions, between August 1962 and December 1964. Australia visibly supported America's military involvement in Vietnam, by dispatching a series of armed advisers and trainers, to the South-East Asian trouble spot. Then, after President Diem and his brother were both assassinated in November 1963, America and Australia noticeably increased their armed support.

Regular soldiers in the AIF quickly joined our existing support groups in South Vietnam, and in 1964 the Australian government introduced conscription for national service. This new policy was never put to a referendum, even though calls for conscription had been rejected twice previously by Australian voters, during the World War 1 era.

Under the new National Service scheme, all Australian 20 year old men were required to register with the Department of Labour and National Service (DLNS). The applicants then became subject to a bi-annual ballot, which, in many ways, resembled a "chook raffle".

If their birth date matched a numbered marble, which was drawn at random from a barrel, the "successful" applicant was selected for compulsory military service. This commitment required two years of continuous full time service in the regular army, followed by three years of part time service with the Army Reserve. A later amendment to the Act, added a crucial new element: Any servicemen involved in full time service, was eligible for special overseas missions.

Those conscripted were notified about their new status within a month, and they then became subject to medical and security examination, before commencing compulsory military training. Twenty-year old Australian men, who failed to register

Prime Minister
Harold Holt

President Lyndon
Johnson

with the DLNS, were automatically considered for "call up", as well as being liable for a fine.

Despite the arbitrary nature of the selection process, over half the population supported these crucial changes in government policy. Indeed general agreement about the conscription process, seemed almost unanimous. When US President, Lyndon Baines Johnson, ("LBJ"), visited Australia on a fleeting good-will visit, large crowds greeted him, and new Prime Minister Harold Holt, declared that,

"Australia was all the way, with LBJ"
By then small anti-war demonstrations were being staged, and in October 1965, sixty protestors were arrested at one "demo". The Federal government, however, remained committed to the conscription policy, and by March 1966, the Australian military task force had been increased to 4,500.

Tragically, in June of that year, Private Errol Noack became the first conscript to be killed in the Vietnam War. Once the body-bag count began to increase on planes returning to Australia, anti-war sentiments steadily became more prevalent.

For the first five years of their involvement, Australian troops were mainly stationed in areas which contained a strong Viet Cong presence. The war environment the Diggers encountered in Vietnam was vastly different to previous military engagements.

Attack from the air

Vietnamese villagers flee an aerial napalm attack

CHAPTER FOURTEEN

TIGERS, TUNNEL RATS AND AGENT ORANGE

Their mascot was a Sumatran tiger cub called "Quintus", but during its tours of duty in Vietnam, the 5th Battalion of the Royal Australian Regiment (RAR), were anything but pussy cats.

The 5th Battalion RAR was first raised at Sydney's Holsworthy Army Base on 3rd March, 1965. Five hundred national servicemen soon swelled its ranks, and some of these newcomers became the first conscripts to serve in Vietnam.

"Quintus", their tiger cub mascot, was presented to the 5th RAR, by the Director of Sydney's Taronga Zoological Park, when troops returned from their first tour of duty to Vietnam. After being added to battalion ranks, "promotion" was rapid for the Sumatran carnivore, and visitors to the picturesque zoo were kept under very close surveillance, by "Lieutenant -Colonel Quintus".

The "Tigers" from the 5th RAR established a proud record during the Vietnam War. Their highly respected Commanding Officer, Lieutenant-Colonel Colin Khan, was awarded a Distinguished Service Order (DSO) after his first

Private Michael
Leahy

tour of duty. In that same year, Major R.F.
Sutton and Second Lieutenant R. A. Brett
both gained a Distinguished Conduct Medal
(DCM). Sergeant W.T. Ward, Corporal M.A.
Dench and Private F.T. Fitch, each collected a
Military Medal (MM), and ten other "Tigers"
of 5 RAR were mentioned in despatches. Sadly
however, 25 casualties were suffered by the 5th
RAR, in active combat situations.

Private Michael "Mick" Francis Leahy
was perilously close to becoming one of "the
Tiger's" fatalities, on his 1969-70 tour of
duty. During Operation Camden, a grenade
exploded behind Mick, which resulted in him
suffering serious shrapnel wounds to his back.
He was moved back to Australia to recuperate, but his injuries prevented him from ever
returning to the South-East Asian conflict.

In civilian life, Mick Leahy always maintained close links with his mates from 5RAR,
before this 62 year old Vietnam War veteran
died from a heart attack in May 2010.

During their initial tour of duty, the 5RAR
Battalion cleared foliage around Nui Dat
before the 1st Australian Task Force established their base. They also participated in
31 battalion sized operations, which included
nine cordons and searches of villages in the
Phouk Tuy province.

On 15th February 1969, the 5th RAR commenced its second tour of duty in the Vietnam War. Their combat role remained of paramount importance. However on this mission, the "Tigers" also involved them selves at "grass roots" level, in the "Pacification Vitalisation" project.

This term incorporated valuable public relations aspects with their military role. Medical practitioners, carpenters, plasterers, concrete workers, cooks and other skilled personnel from the battalion, utilised their various skills to improve the quality of life in villages.

Operationally, the 5th RAR also experienced impressive success on their 1969-1970 tour of duty. They participated in 16 major operations, the most vital of which occurred at Binh Ba. The enemy force was defeated there, and victory at Binh Ba, is still regarded as being a major AIF achievement in the Vietnam War.

Some of the locals, who were evacuated safely from Binh Ba, later proved to be enemy soldiers dressed in civilian clothes, which they had stolen from deserted houses. Such role changes occurred frequently, and identifying the enemy proved to be an ongoing problem in the Vietnam conflict.

The enemy, who became so life threatening at night, could well be a helpful and smiling villager by day. Viet Cong soldiers were almost invisible, for they wore no distinctive uniform. Furthermore, they were often based in complex series of underground tunnels, which were well camouflaged at ground level. Whole communities went about their daily lives on various tiers of their underground settlements. Some had their own hospitals, caches of weapons were often stored there, and entrances were heavily booby trapped.

Battle of Long Tan

Australian soldier John Thompson
at Viet Cong tunnel
(Above right)

Tunnel Rats

Soldiers crossing river searching for Viet Cong positions

Wounded soldier at the Battle of Long Tan

The Allies needed to adjust to this new battle zone phenomenon. Consequently, Australian soldiers assigned to the 3 Field Troop, and 1, 2 and 3 Troop of the 1 Field Squadron of the Royal Australian Engineers (RAE) in Vietnam, became Tunnel Rats. Information from their regular newsletter, "Holdfast", clearly states that only soldiers, who served with one of the above Field Troops, can justifiably refer to themselves as Tunnel Rats.

In this role, they lived "out bush" for four to six weeks, operating as infantry soldiers, and carrying out specialised duties of mine and booby trap detection, tunnel searching, and demolition and bomb disposal. It was not unusual for Tunnel Rats to blow up 100 enemy bunkers in a single operation.

These incredibly courageous Aussie soldiers, often operated in claustrophobic, subterranean environments, with only a hand-gun, torch or bayonet to protect them. The Tunnel Rats are as justifiably proud and protective of their title, as the Rats of Tobruk were of their nickname, during World War 11 combats.

John "Jethro" Thompson was a Tunnel Rat. Initially he worked as a plant operator in Vietnam, but he was still a member of a Field Group, which was then duty bound to support its infantry section. The RAE's motto in C Company, was "wear the badge, do the job". Consequently, while John's usual duties were connected with road building, he was also assigned to Tunnel Rat operations on three occasions.

John Thompson was born in Malta, and relocated to Australia with his Maltese mother and English born father in 1957. The family settled in the Melbourne suburb of Glenroy, and John first worked in a sheet metal factory, after leaving school at an early age.

In 1964 John Thompson enlisted in the Australian Army. A year later he served in Sabah, British North Borneo, before being posted to the Vietnam I Field Squadron of the RAE, in January 1967.

Sadly, four months after his tunnel experience described later in this chapter, John Thompson trod on a land mine at Dat Do. Two of Thompson's comrades were killed in the blast, and his own serious injuries caused him to become a triple amputee.

John "Jethro" Thompson

John Thompson then received extensive medical treatment for 18 testing months, both at Melbourne's Heidelberg Repatriation Hospital, and the Maryport Rehabilitation Centre in Mt. Martha. After his treatment ended, John became a student at Taylor's Coaching College in Melbourne, where he gained his Leaving Certificate. By 1970 he was an administrative officer in the Victorian Public Service, and in the following year John Thompson married his first wife, Judy. The couple were raising a family of five, when Judy tragically died of bowel cancer in 1975. In 1978 he re-married, and since then, John and Perle have raised their blended family in Brisbane.

In Queensland, John Thompson became an active volunteer in the ex-serviceman community, and in 1989 he received an Australia Day Achievement Award. Other honours have since followed. In 1991 John was made a Life Member of the Vietnam Veteran's Association. This was followed by an Order of Australia Medal (OAM) in 2006, in recognition of his outstanding service to war veterans.

The tense incident in an enemy tunnel, which John Thompson graphically describes below, occurred in March-April of 2007, when he was attached to the 6th Battalion C Company for Operation Portsea in Vietnam.

In this mission, in Phuk Quie Province, Thompson's platoon traversed the most gruelling terrain imaginable. At times they were chest-deep in mud, as they forced their way through a swamp, and after they reached firm ground, a forward scout had a daunting assignment in store. An enemy soldier had been sighted disappearing into a weapon pit, and he needed to be found. John Thompson was chosen for the mission, and he describes his terrifying experience in an enemy tunnel in these terms.

"With bayonet in hand, I cautiously approached the narrow opening, feeling and looking for any suspicious signs, before lowering myself into the darkened space.

I had no torch or pistol for protection, (but), feeling with my free hand, and tapping into the immediate area with the bayonet, ... I ventured into the dark tunnel.

...In total darkness I moved forward,... feeling clammy all over, and my breathing started to falter.

Suddenly, my hand was on something. I had no idea what it was. Initially, I thought it was a snake, but it did not move.

What could it be? It was round, loose to touch, and

appeared to be rather long.

Fear was rapidly kicking in. I prodded it gently with my bayonet; there was no reaction. I could hear my breathing getting louder.

Alone and shit scared, I lay quietly listening to my heart pounding away. I needed to be getting out of this claustrophobic place. Steeling myself for an unpleasant reaction, I grabbed it firmly and retreated.

Finally, at the tunnel entrance, I could see that it was nothing more than a long bag of rice that had been carried around the body of an enemy soldier.

Corporal Laurie Drinkwater took my photo, as I climbed out and rested on the enemy weapon pit."

(This extract appears in a fascinating book written by John Thompson, "A Vietnam Vet's Remarkable Life".)

**

Underground warfare in Vietnam was indeed a traumatic experience, but danger also came from the skies, in the form of an insidious new form of weapon, code named Agent Orange.

This form of scientific warfare was a toxic spray, which was dispersed by American planes over enemy forest territory and farm lands. A major aim of this herbicidal and defoliate warfare program was to destroy local protective vegetation cover for the Viet Cong.

However by 1967, disturbing reports began to surface about the long term health effects of Agent Orange, as well as other dangerous defoliates. Some Vietnamese spokesmen later claimed that the Agent Orange program killed thousands of people, and ruined the long term health of many more.

Fears about this chemical weapon, were shared by both serving Australian troops, and their loved ones back in Australia. The widespread anxiety which developed about Agent Orange, was captured vividly by John Schuman's song, "I was only Nineteen"

"And can you tell me doctor, why I still can't get to sleep?
And night-time's just a jungle dark and a barking M.16,
And what's this rash that comes and goes;
Can you tell me what it means?
God help me, I was only nineteen".

U.S. Huey helicopter spraying Agent Orange over Vietnam

In other aspects, the Diggers serving in Vietnam experienced superior conditions to their World War 1 and World War 11 predecessors. Medical back-up was excellent, and the "Wallaby

Airlines", (Canberra bombers), received high praise from soldiers on the front line.

Leisure time for the troops in Vietnam also contained more highlights. While the battle for Long Tan raged not far away, off-duty Aussie soldiers attended a concert which featured "Little Pattie", and other musical celebrities of that era.

Thursday, 18th August 2011, marked the 45th anniversary of the Battle of Long Tan, which is often regarded as being Australia's most decisive contribution in the Vietnam War.

In this encounter, combat was not restricted to underground skirmishes, as the Battle of Long Tan was mostly fought in a large rubber plantation. The Australian's D Company of 6RAR numbered 108 Diggers, and approximately half of them were "Nashos" (conscripted soldiers). They were opposed by an enemy which boasted numbers of between 500 and 1500 troops.

Despite the disparity in numbers, the gallant Diggers doggedly held off the enemy until A Company fortuitously arrived, and victory was achieved. The Aussie defence was greatly assisted by its effective long range artillery, which bombarded significant targets four kilometres from their weapon posts.

Eighteen Australians were KIA at Long Tan, but the enemy casualty rate was close to 250. The US government presented Australia's D Company with a Silver Star award, in recognition of the valour they displayed.

By mid February 1968, when the brutal Tet offensive in South Vietnam showed little sign of being curbed, the Australian Prime Minister, John Gorton, announced there would be no further increase in our troop numbers. Public disenchantment with the long war was then growing, and an August opinion poll revealed that a small majority of Australians wanted our troops to be returned home.

A little over a year later, USA began withdrawing its combat troops out of Vietnam, and in August 1971, William McMahon, Australia's next Prime Minister, belatedly followed the American example.

By then anti-war demonstrations were attracting huge crowds of up to 100,000 people in major Australian cities. Instances of ugly violence at these gatherings, clearly showed that Australia had become a bitterly divided nation over the conscription policy.

In short, the issue had become a social and political disaster, and in December 1972, the Australian Labor Party, (ALP), which had campaigned strongly against our involvement in Vietnam, scored a resounding victory in the Federal elections.

Many volunteer and conscripted soldiers felt bewildered and embittered by the dramatic change in public opinion, which occurred during the decade they fought in that South-East Asian trouble spot. They believed, with much justification, that they were unfairly blamed for being involved, in what became a protracted and unwinnable war.

Four decades on, the scars remain for many of these returned servicemen. A significant number of Vietnam "vets" still suffer long term mental health problems. In fact one reportedly suffered a nervous breakdown, 30 years after being involved in the controversial conflict.

It is estimated that 521 Australian servicemen were KIA in Vietnam, while over 3,000 were injured.

CHAPTER FIFTEEN

VIETNAM VALOUR

Four Australian servicemen were awarded VCs in the Vietnam War. They are noted below in alphabetical order, together with their citation details and some biographical information.

Major Peter John Badcoe (1934-1967): He was member of the Australian Army Training Team, Vietnam. Between 23rd February and 7th April 1967, Badcoe was involved in dangerous military activity at Thua Thien, in the Hue Province of South Vietnam (now the Socialist Republic of Vietnam).

In February 1967, Major Badcoe was working as an adviser to a regional force company, when he monitored radio details about the plight of two American colleagues. The information he received was that an adviser had been KIA, and a medical officer wounded.

Badcoe ignored heavy artillery fire around him, as he traversed the dangerous 600 metre journey to where the two American casualties were stationed. He attended to the wounds of the medical officer, and ensured that he was in safe care.

Major Peter
John Badcoe

Major Badcoe then organised a platoon to attack the enemy. A machine gun post near the dead American adviser was captured, and during the successful operation, Badcoe killed the communist gun crew. Despite being endangered by constant bombardment, the brave Digger carried the corpse of his comrade back to the command centre.

On 7th March, Major Badcoe led another brave charge which turned almost certain defeat into a stirring victory. Unfortunately, on April 7th, Major Peter Badcoe was KIA when he was again leading his company against strong opposition forces. He died at the age of 33.

The Adelaide born Peter Badcoe was born with the surname of Badcock, which he changed in 1961 to Badcoe. His nickname of "the galloping Major" reflected his energetic lifestyle, as Peter Badcoe tackled all his pursuits with boisterous enthusiasm. He represented South Australia in hockey, his first car was a red MG, and in battle he loved to wear a colourful beret.

In May 2008, Peter Badcoe's medals and memoirs were jointly purchased at auction by Network Seven Chief, Kerry Stokes, and the South Australian Government, for a "bargain basement" cost of $488,000. Today his VC medal is housed in Canberra's National War Museum.

Previously, in 1956, Peter Badcoe married Denise McMahon, in the Sydney suburb of Manly. This Vietnam VC winner is survived by his wife, and three daughters.

Warrant Officer Class Two, Keith Payne, VC, OAM. (1933-) Payne was attached to the Australian Training Team, Vietnam, which became involved in dangerous action in the Kontum Province, South Vietnam, on 24th May, 1969.

Keith Payne

Warrant-Officer Payne was commanding the 212th Company of the Mobile Strike Force Battalion, when they were attacked by a numerically stronger North Vietnamese Unit. Payne's unit began to falter under intense fire, until he kept the enemy at bay with an Armalite rifle and grenade attack. In his brave stand, Warrant Officer Payne received hand, arm and hip wounds, from rocket and missile shrapnel.

He still assisted a planned withdrawal from the danger area, by covering his departing men with further grenade and rifle assaults. Then, with the help of a small team he assembled, Keith Payne established a defensive perimeter 350 metres short of an enemy held hilltop area.

That night Keith Payne again returned to the battle area. Despite being once more under heavy fire, he located around 40 Aussie soldiers

who, in the heat of battle had been cut off from the main group. Payne organised the rescue of many of his comrades, and personally assisted in the evacuation of the wounded. It was noted that the inspirational Warrant-Officer dragged some to safety, but others more seriously wounded were carried to safety on his back. Payne gradually recovered from his own wounds and illnesses, after being evacuated back to Brisbane.

Keith Payne was raised in the North Queensland town of Ingham, where he became an apprentice cabinet maker, before enlisting in the AIF at the age of 18. Between 1952 and 1953 he served in the Korean conflict. In 1954 he married Florence Plaw, who was also engaged in military service, with the Women's Royal Australian Army Corps, (RAAC).

As a Corporal, Keith Payne served in both Malaysia and Borneo, and during these tours of duty, he became first a Sergeant, and later a Warrant Officer Class 11. In 1970 Keith Payne served as an instructor at the Duntroon Military Camp near Canberra, and he retired from Australian army life in 1975. The career military man "soldiered on" however, and briefly served as a Captain with the Army of the Sultan of Oman in the Dhofar War. Payne and his wife raised five sons, and they now reside in the Queensland town of Mackay. In 2006 Keith Payne was awarded an Order of Australia Medal, (OAM), for his services to the veteran community.

Payne knew the recently deceased Ted Kenna well, but now Ben Roberts-Smith, Mark Donaldson and he, are the only current Australian VC winners who are still living. Recently all three were honoured guests, when the Hall of Valour was officially opened, at Canberra's National War Museum.

Keith Payne is also much respected for his counselling

work, with war veterans who suffer from post-traumatic stress disorders.

Warrant Officer Class Two, Rayene (Ray) Stewart Simpson (1926-1978): Simpson was also assigned to the Australian Army Training Team, Vietnam. The team was involved in fierce encounters in Kontum Province, South Vietnam, on both the 6th and 11th May, 1969.

Rayene Stewart Simpson

Visibility was very poor in rainy conditions, when the 43 year old Warrant Officer Simpson's unit, was moving through thick bamboo near the Vietnam border. One of the Australian platoons was suddenly subjected to a fierce attack, which badly wounded many, including Warrant Officer M.W. Gill, the commander of the group. Despite being under heavy fire himself, Simpson carried Gill to safety, before returning to the fray, and bombarding the enemy with grenades from close range.

Five days later, Warrant Officer A.M. Kelly, the Commander of the 231st Company, was injured, while his American counterpart, (Captain Green), was killed in another intense engagement. Ray Simpson aided the rescue of many casualties, by providing covering fire.

The wounded were then evacuated from the danger area by helicopter. Once again Simpson was in the fore front of the action, returning fire with the enemy, and thwarting their efforts to abort air evacuation.

Ray Simpson is one of Australia's most experienced and decorated soldiers. The bluntly spoken but compassionate combat veteran, served in World War 11, Korea, the Malaysian emergency and in three tours of Vietnam. In 1964, on his second tour of duty in Vietnam, Ray Simpson was awarded a Distinguished Conduct Medal, (DCM), after he held off an enemy advance, despite suffering severe wounds himself.

After concluding his term of duty in Vietnam, Ray Simpson resided in Japan. In 1952 he married his beloved Shoko, a Japanese woman he first met during the Korean War campaign.

Unfortunately, the Sydney-born VC hero contracted cancer, and he was 52 years of age, when he died in Tokyo.

Kevin Arthur Wheatley

Warrant Officer Class Two, Kevin Arthur "Dasher" Wheatley (1937-1965): Warrant Officer Wheatley was assigned to three companies, on a tour of duty around Tar Bong Valley, in Quant Ngaio Province, South Vietnam, on 13th November, 1965.

Wheatley, and his fellow Warrant Officer, R. W. Swanton, were in charge of three companies on a search and destroy mission. In the afternoon of that day, Warrant Officer Wheatley requested assistance, and he was then joined in the combat by Captain Fazekas and 15 other soldiers.

Another message from Wheatley, informed the captain that Warrant Officer Swanton had received life threatening chest wounds, and he made a further request for an air strike on the enemy, as well as air evacuation for his wounded mate.

Such actions were not immediately possible, and Wheatley was instructed to abandon the seriously injured man, and return to a safe position, This order was ignored. Instead "Dasher" Wheatley discarded his heavy radio, and half-dragged and half-carried the wounded Swanton through heavy fire, from an open rice field into the relative safety of a wooded area.

At this stage, a South Vietnamese Private again urged Wheatley to abandon his fast dying comrade, but once more the advice went unheeded. When the advancing Viet Cong troops circled to within ten metres of the defiant pair, Wheatley was last seen holding two live grenades in his hands.

Next morning Captain Fazekas discovered both men's shot bodies. Wheatley, who chose certain death in order to support his wounded digger mate, was awarded a posthumous VC.

"Dasher" Wheatley was the son of a Sydney labourer, and he had an assortment of unskilled jobs, before he enlisted in the army at the age of 19. Two years previously, he had married 14 year old Edna, and the couple raised four children. By reputation, Kevin Wheatley was a rough, wild man, and his nickname of "Dasher", originated from his Rugby Union background.

Wheatley previously served in Malaysia, and this short, stocky and popular knock-about character, was a highly regarded soldier. A sports arena in Vietnam was named after the brave Warrant Officer. Kevin "Dasher Wheatley was only 28 years of age when he was KIA.

VC recipients Corporal Mark Donaldson, Corporal Ben Roberts-Smith and Mr Keith Payne and in Perth, Australia (2011)

CHAPTER SIXTEEN

RECENT CONFLICTS IN THE MIDDLE EAST AND AFGHANISTAN

Between August 2nd 1991, and February 28th 1992, armed conflict was waged in the oil rich Middle Eastern country of Kuwait. A United Nations coalition of 34 nations, headed by USA, responded to Iraq's annexation of their small, neighbouring country, by launching a military operation code named "Desert Storm" against the invader.

Australia did not send combat troops to the Gulf War, but our government of the time played a significant role in the United Nations response. We shared responsibility for ensuring that sanctions imposed on Iraq were effective, and we also provided overall assistance to the Desert Storm response.

Eleven years later our reaction was more decisive, when America invaded Iraq. Prime Minister John Howard strongly supported President George W. Bush's military moves to disarm Iraq, and oust the country's leader, Saddam Hussein.

Prime Minister John
Howard

President George
W. Bush

Howard described Hussein's leadership as being **"A dictatorship of a particularly horrific kind"**, and pointed to the removal of basic human rights for many in Iraq, under the despot's cruel leadership. Both the American and Australian Governments became strongly focussed on destroying the alleged "weapons of mass destruction" (WMD), which they believed Saddam Hussein had stockpiled in secret locations around Iraq.

Some critics claimed that Australia only sent token numbers of our military personnel to Iraq, to demonstrate solidarity with America's commitment. Others believed that both America's and Australia's chief motivating factor, was the protection of the region's rich oil reserves, which are vital for the economies of the Western world. Such sceptics also highlighted the fact that two UN experts could find no evidence that WMD existed in Iraq.

Despite such misgivings, there is no doubting the initial strength of Australia's involvement. As the conflict continued to escalate, we became one of the "top four" nations in contributions to the war effort.

Three Royal Australian Navy (RAN) ships, 500 Special Force soldiers, a P3 Orion Maritime Patrol Aircraft, a C 130 Hercules Transport aircraft, and Number 75 Squadron of the Royal Australian Air Force (RAAF), with 14 F/A-18 Hornet Fighters, were all assigned for active duty in the Iraq War.

In addition, three combat units were deployed in the conflict, and by 2005 our ground troops, and Iraqi security forces, became responsible for maintaining control in the less dangerous southern provinces. Many Australian troops were wounded in the invasion of Iraq, but fortunately none were KIA.

By 2007, however, many Australians had become disillusioned with the conduct of the war. The Howard Government, which had not wavered in its military involvement to the controversial conflict, lost power in the Federal election of that year. The newly elected Labor Government, which had mounted a spirited anti-war campaign, gradually commenced withdrawing our troops from Iraq. By late July, 2009, only a token Australian force remained.

September 11

America's military involvement in Afghanistan has its roots in a terrorist attack on September 11th 2001, which sent shock tremors through America, and indeed the entire world. On that terrible day, a terrorist gang of 19 Arab extremists murdered nearly 3,000 people, in four separate suicide attacks in New York, Washington DC, and Pennsylvania. Even before the final death toll was known, President George W. Bush echoed the shock and rage of his countrymen, when he vowed

"We will make no distinction between the terrorists

who committed these acts, and those who harbour them."

Within a month, America showed that it had zero tolerance with any countries which welcomed terrorists, and Afghanistan undoubtedly had a reputation of being a safe haven for enemies of the West. Consequently, once Bush became convinced that Osama bin Laden, the suspected master-mind of the September 11 atrocities, was hiding in remote areas of that rugged and mountainous country, America landed military forces in Afghanistan. The invasion was never sanctioned by the UN Security Council.

Australia was quick to honour its alliance obligations to USA, and terrorist attacks on our own citizens around that time, only hardened our resolve. On October 12th, 2002, 88 Aussies were killed in horrific terrorist attacks at nearby Bali. After that tragedy, it became a priority for us to protect both our nation, and any individual Australians travelling abroad, from any threats of international terrorism.

By then three Australian Special Force squadrons had been deployed in military operations against Taliban opponents in Afghanistan, and our diggers featured prominently in the capture of Kandahar airport. In September 2005, Special Force Units were redeployed, and in the early months of 2007, two Chinook helicopters were sent to the battle zones to assist the Special Force operation.

Since August 2006, our main involvement in Afghanistan has been focused in Uruzgan Province. Already there have been four Reconstruction Task Forces which have erected and re-built essential services for local people. Our troops have also attacked Taliban command and supply centres in the province.

U.S. Soldiers at the Afganistan War

After 2014, when Australia originally planned to withdraw its main military presence from Afghanistan, local Afghan forces will take complete responsibility for safeguarding their country. Consequently, an ongoing priority for our military personnel, has been to act as mentors for local defence units. Such training, it is hoped, will result in a smooth transfer of power, when Afghans assume sole responsibility for the protection of their democratically elected government.

However by early November 2011, this laudable instruction policy came under serious threat from a new and difficult problem. In late May of that year, 25 year old Corporal Andrew Jones from Queensland was gunned down and killed by Shafied Ullah, an Afghan National Army soldier, who had been sharing patrol duties with the young Australian. The renegade ally was himself slain a few weeks later, by US and Afghan Special Forces.

Then, on Saturday 29th October 2011, three Australian soldiers from the 2nd Battalion RAR were killed, and seven colleagues wounded, when a trainee Afghani Sergeant machine gunned them from behind, on the parade ground at Tarin Kowt. Twenty-two year old Corporal Ashley Birt, 27 year old

Lance-Corporal Luke Gavin and 26 year old Captain Bryce Duffy were killed, while another seriously wounded Australian digger was air lifted to a German military hospital. Two other Australian soldiers shot dead the assailant, following the cowardly surprise attack.

Such worrying instances of *déjà vu* have continued. On Tuesday 8th November 2011, three other Australian soldiers were wounded when Mohammed Roozi, another rogue Afghan National Army soldier, opened fire on his fellow troops in the Charmestan region. The assailant then fled into rugged country in an army vehicle, before an intense search for the culprit could be mounted. The injuries sustained by the young diggers was described as "serious, but not life threatening". Afghan National troops, who were serving with their Australian mentors, were temporarily relieved of their weapons.

In February 2012, the still uncaptured Roozi boasted about his cowardly attack on a video released by the Taliban, claiming that he **"..had one mission on my mind - to kill foreigners and teach them a lesson."**

Scene from Afganistan

Roozi also warned Allied forces that he was not the only Afghan soldier who harboured murderous thoughts about Western mentors, a worrying claim which was quickly dismissed by an Australian Defence Force (ADF) spokeswoman.

Julia Gillard

Australia's Prime Minister, Julia Gillard had previously admitted that such incidents "do corrode trust". Currently 33 Australian servicemen have lost their lives in the Afghanistan conflict. Furthermore, the three cowardly attacks on seven Australian soldiers between May and November in the Tarin Kowt Province, raised an obvious question for the voting public.

How can Australia continue to support the war effort in Afghanistan, when our soldiers are being continually ambushed by the Afghan troops we are training?

Both major Federal political parties have bi-partisan support for our continuing military commitment in this war. However in recent times the general public has become increasingly disillusioned about Australia's involvement in the conflict. On Remembrance Day 2011, a "Melbourne Age" Readers' Poll revealed that 81% of those who participated in a opinion survey, want Australian troops to leave Afghanistan as quickly as possible.

Our allies in the conflict appear to have similar misgivings. In August 2010, the

Netherlands withdrew from their joint commitment with Australia in the Uruzgan Province. More recently, in late January 2012, Nicolas Sarkosy, then the President of France, threatened to withdraw all French troops from Afghanistan by 2013, which is 12 months short of France's original commitment.

This abrupt change of attitude occurred, after four French troops were killed by a renegade Afghani soldier they were training. By then 82 servicemen from France had been killed in the Afghanistan conflict, and 82% of the French general public favoured an end to their country's military commitment in that troubled country.

Around the same time, opinion polls in America indicated that 70% of the public wanted their troops returned home. By then at least 1,900 Americans had been killed in the decade long conflict, and a large majority of voters believed that USA's participation in the Afghanistan war had been a mistake from the outset. It now seems more likely, that strong disillusionment about the protracted and seemingly unsuccessful war, will finally change the Obama government's original withdrawal deadline.

On February 3rd 2012, US Defence Secretary, Leon Panetta, unexpectedly announced that the American combat mission in Afghanistan, could end as soon as mid 2013, which is at least a year earlier than first intended.

This surprising development appeared to impact on the Australian government's policy. In April 2012, Prime Minister Gillard announced that many Diggers serving in Afghanistan would return home by August 2013, - a year in advance of our previous deadline.

"By then," the Prime Minister asserted, **"we will have completed our training and mentoring mission."**

Julia Gillard also claimed that recent gains by the Allied forces, (such as the killing of Osama bin Laden), had brought significant improvements within the war torn country, and that Afghanistan had become a safer country within the past 18 months.

Tony Abbott, the Opposition leader in Federal Parliament, appears to have provided cautious bi-partisan support to this change of policy, so the majority of our serving troops may be back in Australia before the next scheduled Federal elections are conducted.

U.S. Forces at Afganistan

CHAPTER SEVENTEEN

AUSSIE HEROES
IN AFGHANISTAN

At present, two Australian servicemen have been awarded VC medals, for displaying conspicuous valour in the Afghanistan War. The recipients, together with their citation details, and some biographical information, are listed below.

Trooper Mark Gregor Strang Donaldson (1979-): A member of a Special Operations Task Force during "Operation Slipper", in Oruzgan Province, Afghanistan, on 2nd September, 2008.

Trooper Donaldson was travelling with a combined Afghan, American and Australian vehicle convoy, which was suddenly ambushed by a large group of Taliban fighters. The allied group was subjected to fierce machine gun and rocket fire, which inflicted heavy casualties. The vehicle convoy completely lost the initiative in this devastating attack, and their advance was suppressed.

During the early stages of the ambush, Trooper Donaldson reacted quickly to revive his group. He moved rapidly between alternative positions of cover, while engaging the enemy in

Trooper Mark
Donaldson

a gun battle. He also deliberately exposed himself to Taliban marksmen, in an effort to draw enemy fire to himself, and away from the wounded soldiers who were being rescued, and removed to the convoy's vehicles.

Soon these trucks and jeeps were so full of wounded soldiers, that Donaldson, and other uninjured comrades, were forced to run alongside the vehicles. There they were again exposed to more heavy enemy fire.

During the retreat, Donaldson noticed that a severely wounded Coalition Force Interpreter was lying 80 metres away, where he was exposed to the Taliban gunners. Donaldson abandoned the forced withdrawal, rushed to his injured mate through a hail of bullets, and carried him to safety. He then successfully applied first aid to the interpreter, and others in the convoy, before returning to the gun battle.

Mark Donaldson was born in the NSW city of Newcastle in 1979, and enlisted in the army in 2002. After completing his course with the Special Air Service Regiment, Donaldson saw active service in East Timor and Iraq, before being assigned to the Afghanistan conflict. In the early days of his term of duty there, Mark Donaldson suffered minor wounds.

The actions which gained Trooper Donaldson a VC in Afghanistan, when he saved one comrade's life, and ensured the safety of many others, were later glowingly described as being **"Conspicuous acts of gallantry, in circumstances of great peril".**

It was the first time in nearly 40 years that an Australian serviceman had been awarded a VC. On 22nd January 2009, only six days after he was officially invested with the VC medal, the 29-year-old Mark Donaldson donated his prestigious award to Canberra's National War Museum for public viewing.

Mark Donaldson is married to Emma, who ruefully declares that **"Mark is married to the army".**

The couple currently have one child, a daughter named Kaylee. The modest and unpretentious young man maintains that **"I don't see myself as a hero, honestly. I still see myself as a soldier, first and foremost".**

Corporal Benjamin Roberts-Smith (1978-): The Patrol Second-In-Command of a Special Operational Task Group, engaged in "Operation Slipper", during a helicopter assault into Kandahar Province, on 11th June, 2010.

The aim of the military operation, was to capture or kill a senior Taliban commander, who was allegedly based in the area.

After arriving by helicopter, the group was subjected to heavy machine gun and rocket detonation attack from multiple positions. Two of the Task Force were wounded. The remainder of the group was pinned down by continual fire from three machine gun positions in elevated and fortified positions, south of the village of Tizac.

However Corporal Roberts-Smith's patrol, despite being subjected to heavy fire from the numerically superior enemy,

Corporal Benjamin
Roberts-Smith

bravely moved to within forty metres of the Taliban's entrenched position. Roberts-Smith then killed an enemy insurgent in a close-quarter encounter, before drawing fire away from his group, by fearlessly exposing his position.

The Corporal's decoy tactics, enabled his Patrol Commander to silence one machine gun post with a successful grenade attack. Ben Roberts-Smith then stormed another machine gun post, and killed the two remaining gunners.

Roberts-Smith's brave and inspiring actions resulted in a crucial break- through into the enemy position, and released his patrol from intense fire. His courageous performance allowed the Task Group seized command of a strong gun position, which they used to kill more opposition forces. Finally, the village of Tizak, and the Shah Wali Kot district, was cleared of Taliban insurgents.

Previously, on his second tour of duty to Afghanistan in May 2006, Ben Roberts- Smith was awarded a Medal of Gallantry (MG), for his feats of bravery near Afghanistan's Chora Pass.

During that skirmish, in harsh and mountainous terrain, the then Lance-Corporal Roberts-Smith maintained an exposed sniper position against large numbers of Taliban insurgents, in order to safeguard his patrol.

Ben Roberts-Smith was born in Perth in 1978 into a high-achieving family. His father, Len, headed the Western Australian Corruption and Crime Commission. Ben's brother, Daniel, is a talented opera singer, who has previously been the recipient of a Joan Sutherland award.

In 1996 Ben enlisted in the AIF. He served with the 3 Royal Australian Regiment (3RAR) in Malaysia, and on two tours of duty in East Timor. In 2003 Roberts-Smith completed a Special Air Service Regiment (SASR) course, before being assigned to the 3 Squadron, which served both in South-East Asia and Fiji.

After receiving his MG award in Afghanistan, Corporal Roberts-Smith became second in command of the 2 Section in 2009.

Ben's VC Medal is the 63rd such award to be displayed in Canberra's National War Museum, and it is now 111 years since the first Australian VC medal was awarded to Captain Neville House. Ben and Emma Roberts-Smith are the proud parents of twin baby daughters, and the tall war hero is motivated by his parental responsibilities, whenever he is engaged in active combat. After he was invested with his VC medal, Ben Roberts-Smith asserted that:

"I want my children to be able to live as everyone does now, (in Australia), without the fear of getting on a bus, and having it blown up."

CHAPTER EIGHTEEN

WOMEN, ABORIGINES AND OTHER UNSUNG WARRIORS

Historically, the roles of women in times of war have been greatly underrated. When husbands are engaged in overseas military service, it is the wives and mothers who usually accept responsibility for raising children, and managing household budgets and resources. Their lives are filled with tension, because of continual concern for their partner's or son's welfare. If their men die on far away battlefields, women sometimes grieve alone.

During World War 1, opportunities arose for women to involve themselves in worthwhile wartime fund raising activities. Organisations such as the Australian Red Cross, the Country Women's Association, (CWA), the Christian Temperance Society, the Australian Women's National League, the Voluntary Aid Detachment, the Australian Comfort Fund and the Cheer- Up Society, all assisted in supporting the war effort on the home front.

Furthermore, involvement in their activities was both socially and emotionally rewarding. Some of these groups, as well as similar modern counterparts, still function effectively today, especially in war time situations.

For over a century, Australian women have also served in overseas battle zones. Ida Robertson, from the NSW country town of Hay, was one of the first volunteer nurses to be involved in front line action in the Boer War. During that South African conflict, Australia suffered its first recorded woman war casualty, when a nursing sister named Frances "Fanny" Emma Hines died of pneumonia on 7th August, 1900.

Before her premature death, Fanny Hines served in some disease infested battle zones, and at one stage she was in sole charge of 26 patients. She is now buried far from home, at the Bulawayo Cemetery, in present day Zimbabwe. Matron E.J. Gould, Sister Penelope Frater and Superintendent Julie Bligh, were other Australian volunteer nurses, who served in the South African conflict.

Towards the end of the Boer War, some volunteer Australian women teachers catered for basic educational needs of the women and children, who were interned as POW's in British concentration camps.

Often the same motivating urges, which influenced their male counterparts, caused Australian women to volunteer for overseas service. Olive King sought adventure by becoming an ambulance driver in France and the Balkans. She saved countless numbers of lives in that demanding role. Vera Deakin, the daughter of former Prime Minister Alfred Deakin, founded a Wounded and Missing Enquiry Bureau in Cairo, and later London. Sister Narelle Hobbs found herself alongside our first

Diggers at Gallipoli. In an extract taken from a letter she wrote, there is no doubting her strong commitment.

"I've been a soldier now for nearly three years, and please God I will go right to the end...if anything happened, and I too passed out, well there would be no finer way in which I would be happier, than to lay down one's life for the men who have given everything."

Vera Deakin

Sister Hobbs died approximately five months later. Two years previously, a group of New South Wales nurses sailed to France to serve on the Western Front. They were decked out in blue uniforms, and became famously known as "The Bluebirds".

It was in that gruesome battle zone in Europe, that four young nurses became the first recipients of war bravery awards for Australian women. Sisters Claire Deacon, Dorothy Cawood and Alice Ross-King, along with Nurse Mary Derrer, were each honoured with a Military Medal (MM), for risking their lives rescuing patients in burning buildings.

Narelle Hobbs

The bombing of the 2nd Australian Casualty Clearing Station at Trois Arbres near Armentieres, occurred at night on 22nd July, 1916. The four nurses ignored patients' pleas to seek shelter in the dug outs during the bombing blitz, and Alice Ross –King injured

Alice Ross –King

herself during the rescue operation, when she fell into a bomb crater, which was hidden in the darkness. Ross-King later provided a graphic diary account about the mayhem which surrounded her, after the first bombs fell.

"Though I shouted, nobody answered me, or I could hear nothing for the roaring of the planes and 'Archies', (artillery). I seemed to be the only living thing about…I kept calling for Wilson, (a medical orderly), to help me, and thought he was funking, but the poor boy had been blown to bits."

Later, when all four of the heroines were recommended for Military Medals, their "coolness and devotion to duty" were especially noted.

Other Australian nurses became MM recipients during World War 1. Rachael Pratt was recommended for that award, when she was nursing on the island of Lemnos near the Gallipoli invasion point. Though her lung was punctured from shrapnel wounds, she kept attending to wounded soldiers, until she collapsed and had to be removed from the scene. Rachael Pratt then endured a long period of recovery, and she still suffered from severe bronchitis for the rest of her life.

Alicia (Rachel) Mary Kelly disobeyed orders and continued to nurse and comfort patients during an intense Western Front air raid. Eileen King was another revered heroine. Part of her thigh broke away, after she was badly injured in an air attack in France, but the gritty nurse still managed to remove wounded patients from a burning tent. Soldiers who observed her actions that day, regard Eileen King as "one of the bravest women they ever met".

Pearl Corkhill

Pearl Corkhill also gained a MM in World War 1, during a July 1917 bombing attack at Longvillers in the Somme. Corkhill displayed admirable calm in the crisis, which greatly helped the morale of wounded soldiers in her care. Later, in a letter to her Sydney- based parents, the shy young woman confided her greatest fear about the MM situation.

"I can't see what I've done to deserve it, but the part I don't like is (meeting) old George, (the King of England), to give me the medal!"

Two thousand, five hundred and sixty-two Australian Army Nursing Service, (AANS), women enlisted for service in World War 1, and 25 of these volunteers were KIA. Most worked in field hospitals, and in medical ships, anchored close to front line action.

On the home front, very few women entered the depleted Australian work force during World War 1. Those who did were mostly restricted to occupations in the food, clothing and printing industries.

The situation changed dramatically in the

World War 11 era, when it became necessary to recruit women into occupations which had been traditionally earmarked for men. Once the war ended, men returned from battle zones to their previous employment. This sudden change caused adjustment problems for many women, who had enjoyed participating in the work force.

Other wartime employment opportunities opened up for women, with the establishment of the Australian Women's Land Army (AWLA). This initiative was established in July 1942, in order to address a chronic labour shortage in country areas. By 1944, approximately 3,000 women workers were employed by the AWLA. Participants did not receive the same financial inducements as WRANS or AWAS, as their work was not considered to be a military service. In World War 11 battle zones, it is recorded that 3,477 AANS women served in World War 11 action, and 71 of these volunteers were KIA.

Career opportunities for women in the armed forces, have improved noticeably in recent years. It is now estimated that 93% of military positions are now available for both men and women applicants, and in future years this anomaly will be removed completely.

On 27th September 2011, Federal Defence Minister, Stephen Smith, announced that the 7% of military positions still currently off-limits for females will become available within the next five years, for any women applicants who meet a decided criteria. At present, New Zealand and Canada are the only other two countries, who have opened up all military roles for women in their defence positions.

This enlightened reform potentially increases the depth of talent in our military capabilities. Natalie Sambhi is just one of many gifted Australian women, who welcomes the new career opportunities which will arise.

Ms. Sambhi, a 29 year old international relations post-graduate who speaks six languages, first applied to become an officer in the reserves in 2009. Against her wishes, she was forced to apply to the signals corps, because women are not allowed to join infantry corps. However within the next five years Natalie Sambhi can expect to not only graduate as an infantry officer who sees front line action; she also has the opportunity to become a combat leader. Sambhi is clearly elated at the prospect.

Natalie Sambhi

"To serve on the front line, to be able to muster an esprit de corps among my soldiers, to be able to lead them, to be able to fight for something I believe in, for my country... it's something I've wanted so badly..." was her enthusiastic response.

Already there are married women with children, who have become pilots, doctors, lawyers and navigators in Australia's defence force, and it is the RAAF which has been the equal opportunity pioneer. In 1984 women personnel were absorbed into the main stream, and four years later the first female Air Force pilots graduated.

More women are now employed in high command positions. Currently, the highest

Elizabeth Cosson

Brigadier Lyn
McDade

ranked woman in the force is Air Vice-Marshall Margaret Staib, who is the commander in charge of logistics. Julie Hammer is another who rose through the ranks to become a Vice- Marshall in the RAAF. The highly decorated Vicki McConachie, (who raised two children and obtained a Masters Law degree), was promoted to the position of Commodore in 2007.

Another female high achiever is Elizabeth (Liz) Cosson, who became Australia's most senior female military officer, and the country's first woman Major General in the AIF. Commodore Robyn Walker and Brigadier Lyn McDade, along with McConchie, are other women who have currently reached the one- star promotional level in the Australian armed forces.

Australia's most enduring female war hero is Nancy Wake, who topped the Gestapo's most wanted list in 1943. To the frustrated enemy, Wake became very much "a lady of immaculate deception." She set up escape routes for thousands of allied soldiers and air-men from dangerous war zones, she led a band of the French Resistance, she became a revered spy and saboteur, and none were more feisty, brave or cunning than this beautiful young woman.

"She is the most feminine woman I know, until the fighting starts," recalled a French

colleague. **"Then she is like five men."**

Nancy Wake was born in a dilapidated weatherboard shack in Wellington, New Zealand. She was the youngest of six children, and was very fond of her filmmaker father, Charles. Consequently, when he moved permanently to USA shortly after the family relocated to Sydney, Nancy was devastated. She ran away from home at the age of 16, and for two years worked under an assumed name as a nurse in Mudgee. She then before returned to Sydney, but set up residence away from her family.

Vicki McConachie

Luckily a timely bequest from a New Zealand aunt, enabled Nancy to travel to London, where she trained as a journalist, and reported on news from England and France. One frequent topic was the sudden popularity of Nazi propaganda in nearby Germany. Nancy Wake soon became a formidable opponent of this new outbreak of Fascist philosophy.

Margaret Staib

In 1936 she met Henri Fiocca, a Marseilles millionaire. The couple married just after World War 11 began, and Nancy soon became appalled by the number of collaborationists who lived comfortably under Nazi rule.

Wake became motivated to act as a courier for the local Resistance movement. She carried everything, including simple messages and sophisticated radio parts, to other partisans. She was often openly flirtatious with German

Nancy Wake

guards, which helped her negotiate check points successfully.

Before long Nancy was taking groups of refugees, grounded Allied pilots and Jewish families from one "safe house" to another, until safety was reached. Her fame spread, and the Gestapo dubbed Nancy Wake "the white mouse", because of her ability to disappear, when it seemed she was within their grasp. On one occasion, enemy bullets were whistling around her ears, before she managed to find her way safely through the Pyrenees.

Her French husband was not as fortunate. Henri was arrested by the Gestapo, and later executed, after he refused to reveal her whereabouts.

"I will go to my grave regretting that," lamented Nancy years later, "For Henri was the love of my life."

Nancy then retuned to London, where she completed 16 weeks of retraining from Britain's well regarded Special Operations Executive. When the intensive course concluded, Nancy Wake was an expert in explosives, weaponry, hand to hand combat, and survival skills behind enemy lines.

In the early hours of March 31st 1943, Nancy was parachuted back into forest land north of Clermont Ferrand in France, where partisan groups numbered close to 7,000. Her goal was to discover the munitions needs of each band, and to relay this information back to London.

However Nancy Wake soon discovered that some of the partisan leaders did not respect her position of authority. A few drinking contests with these "macho" men, made them see her in a new light, as "the white mouse" was always the "last man standing" at the end of drunken binges.

When D Day arrived on 6th June 1944, Nancy's life was totally absorbed with ambushing Germans, blowing up bridges, wrecking trains and narrowly escaping death. Her French partisan supporters came to idolise the warrior-like capabilities of the foreign leader they dubbed "Madame Andree".

"Madame Andree is braver than Jacques," commented one partisan to a British OBE recipient, "and Jacques is the bravest of us all."

On one raid, Wake killed an SS sentry with her bare hands, by slitting his throat, before he could alert colleagues about the presence of resistance forces. In another escapade, "the white mouse" reportedly covered 800 kilometres on her bicycle, in order to replace wireless codes, which had been discovered by the enemy.

Her French partisan groups gained notable victories. Vichy was liberated from Marshall Petain's collaborationist groups, and Wake herself was one of the first to enter Paris, when German resistance began to crumble.

In the Paris-based British Officers' Club, "the white mouse" became "the mouse that roared", in a confrontation with a haughty waiter. The man thought he had won an argument, when he stated that he would rather serve Germans, than her boisterous group. Nancy then erupted into action.

In a matter of seconds, she leapt to her feet and knocked the waiter senseless with a right hook. When another concerned waiter rushed to his colleague's side with a glass of brandy, it was Nancy who gratefully drained the contents. She then politely murmured "Merci", before leaving the premises.

Nancy Wake received many honours for her wartime feats, including the Congressional Medal of Freedom from USA, the George Medal from Britain, and the Legion d' Honneur, the Croix de Guerre and the Medaille de la Resistance from France. Controversially, however, five decades elapsed before an Australian government awarded her a medal.

The premise underpinning this decision was simple: Nancy Wake had not fought for any of the Australian armed services during World War 11. In more recent years, Federal governments approached her about belatedly accepting an Australian award, but such attempts were consistently refused. Wake, in typically abrasive style, provided reasons for her attitude in April 2000.

"The last time there was a suggestion about giving me an Australian medal, I told the government that they could stick their medals where the monkey stuck his nuts. The thing is, if they gave me a medal now, it wouldn't be given with love, so I don't want anything from them. They can bugger off!"

Eventually, in 2004, the Australian government made Nancy Wake a Companion of the Order of Australia, which is one of many of her awards now on display at Canberra's National War Museum.

Once World War 11 ended, Wake felt dissatisfied and restless in normal civilian life. She campaigned for the Liberal

Party in two general elections, and came close to toppling the Labor stalwart, Dr. Hubert Evatt. She then remarried, and settled with her ex-RAAF husband, John Forward, in Port Macquarie on the NSW central coast. After he died in 1997, Nancy relocated to London in 2001 to be near old comrades. She was 98 years of age, when she died on August 7th, 2011.

Australian writer, Peter FitzSimons, compiled her colourful life story in the twilight of her days, and in one discussion, she confided her burial wishes to her biographer.

"I want to be cremated, and I want my ashes to be scattered over the mountains where I fought with the Resistance. That will be good enough for me."

Julia Gillard, Australia's Prime Minister at the time of the war heroine's death, provided the following eulogy:

"Nancy Wake was a woman of exceptional courage and resourcefulness, whose daring exploits saved the lives of hundreds of allied personnel, and helped bring the Nazi occupation of France to an end."

**

Women heroes from Australia also emerged in the Pacific Ocean battle zones of World War 11. When the ship "Empire Star" was bombed during the fall of Singapore, Vera Torney and Margaret Anderson used their own bodies to shield wounded fellow passengers from Japanese bombing attacks. Following their fearless actions, Torney received a Member of the British Empire (MBE) award, while Anderson was awarded a George Medal.

**

"Man's inhumanity to man, makes countless thousands mourn" (Robbie Burns)

Hideous war crimes were committed, but some remarkable World War 11 Australian heroines came to the fore, in the Banka Strait, an area which is now part of present day Indonesia. Originally, in February 1942, there were 65 Australian nurses assembled on a doomed hospital ship in the area, but by the time survivors reached Fremantle nearly four years later, only 24 of the women were able to disembark.

The saga began on 12th February 1942, when a small, coastal steamer named "Vyner Brooke" was bombed by three Japanese planes. The luckless passengers on board were mostly attached to the Australian Nursing Army Service (ANAS). Twelve of these 65 nurses drowned, or were killed in the ocean, when they were forced to abandon ship.

After spending as long as 60 hours in the water, the exhausted survivors managed to reach Banka Island, a remote outpost, which is approximately 140 kilometres long and 60 kilometres wide. They decided their only option was to surrender to Japanese soldiers stationed on the island. Unfortunately, this decision resulted in severe hardship and even death.

Two groups of male captives were escorted away from the others. Soon after gun shots were heard, and the men failed to re-appear. Tommy Lloyd was wounded, but he did manage to rush into the sea, and escape the Tommy gun executions. Lloyd subsequently became a POW, and in later years he provided authorities with an account, of what transpired on that horrendous day.

Twenty-three nurses were also ordered to wade into the

water, where all but one was massacred. In fact the Australian women had only advanced a few metres into the waves, when they were machine gunned from behind. Sister Vivian Bullwinkle from South Australia was shot in the side. However she miraculously survived the Banka Straits Massacre, by lying still in the salt water, until her murderous attackers vacated the area. She later re-lived her terrifying experience

Vivian Bullwinkle

"I saw the girls fall one after another... Then I was hit...It, (the bullet), missed all the organs...Later I took myself into the jungle...I knew what happened to everyone else...I did find a tin of condensed milk, but I had no way of opening it".

For a few days Bullwinkle, and a male fugitive called Kingsley, survived on supplies provided by villagers. Kingsley turned 39 during his brief time of freedom, but he died soon afterwards. Bullwinkle was then forced surrender again to the Japanese. During her long period in detention, she never directly referred to the horrific war crimes which occurred in Banka Strait, for fear of further reprisals.

Bullwinkle and other nurse captives in the settlement were given the option of becoming sex workers in a brothel. After that offer was refused, they were at first housed with Dutch women and children in the poorer part of town, where there was inadequate sanitation and little food.

Their situation became even more desperate. Soon they were shifted to jungle accommodation, where trench toilets reeked, and huts leaked in wet weather. After moving again, four more Australian nurses died through lack of medical care. One of the four fatalities, Sister Pearl Mitteheuser, lingered on until 18th August 1945. In a cruel twist of fate, she died three days after Japanese forces officially surrendered.

By then the nurses were imprisoned in Sumatra, where diseases such as malaria, beri beri and dysentery were rife. The "fittest" members of the group often had to transport weaker members on stretchers, Finally, at Loebock Linggauin, living conditions for the prisoners reached their lowest ebb. There the 500 inmates lived in overcrowded huts, and water had to be carried from a creek.

Agnes "Betty" Jeffrey, a captive nurse, later wrote about her traumatic POW experiences in a book titled "White Coolies". In the contents she describes how the starving women in captivity, managed to survive.

Agnes "Betty" Jeffrey

"We find we can eat most of the grass growing near the creek; also the young, curling ferns. Curried ferns with sweet potato, are like eating mushrooms."

Despite their weakened physical well state, Betty Jeffrey maintained that

"We never lost our spirit, even if we lost our strength".

Facts bear out the brave woman's defiant assertion. Some of the POWs composed a song titled "Song of Survival", and 30 Australian, Dutch and British women prisoners shared lipstick and "best" clothes, before presenting this ditty, and other musical items, at well attended camp concerts. Those on stage mostly stayed seated during their performance: they were too physically weak to stand. The popular concerts were regularly staged throughout 1944, even though half of the original performers died during that same year.

Though the war was drawing to a close, Australian authorities had by then lost all contact with the nurses. Unfortunately they were overlooked, when food and medical supplies were dropped from planes, and by August 1944 they faced the grim prospect of starving to death.

However, after Japan surrendered on 15th August 1945, an Australian war correspondent named Hayden Lennard, began searching for the lost nurses. Information provided by local villagers, finally led him to their primitive dwellings at Loebok Linggau, where he discovered 24 emaciated survivors.

A month later, the rescued nurses were greeted at Singapore's Changi International Airport by a welcoming delegation headed by Colonel Annie Sage. The group was shocked to see that only a few of the original 65 nurses survived their gruelling three years and seven months imprisonment. Harry Windsor, an Australian army doctor at the airport, later commented that the Japanese perpetrators responsible for their imprisonment should be **"... slowly and**

painfully butchered."

By then Sister Betty Jeffery, (who was of average height), weighed only 30 kilograms, and was suffering badly from tuberculosis. Sister Bullwinkle, whose hair had largely fallen out during the ordeal, later attended war trials of some accused Japanese. She felt severely traumatised once more, after she heard the same language and accents, which had formerly been spoken by her cruel captors.

It was the 25th October 1945, when the surviving 24 army nurses finally arrived safely in Fremantle on the hospital ship, "Manunda". They looked emaciated from their harrowing experiences, but the grateful survivors all emphasised strongly with their colleague, Sylvia Muir, who emotionally declared on arrival that **"It was lovely, it was Australia; I just started to howl"**.

Experienced wartime observers maintained that the Japanese atrocities committed in the Banka Strait region were the worst example of war crimes against humanity. It was the 229th Regiment of the 38th Japanese Division, which was responsible for the cowardly massacre of the 22 nurses, and after World War 11 ended, the search began for the war criminals who committed the mass murders.

Lieutenant Masayuki Takeuchi was jailed in Malaya after being identified in a POW stockade, while Sergeant-Major Tarokato was captured in New Guinea. Overall, however, arresting suspects was a difficult operation, as many in that Japanese regiment lost their lives after the massacre, in battles fought in the Solomon Islands. Ultimately no prosecutions were made by the International War Crimes Tribunal, which heard evidence in Tokyo

Vivian Bullwinkle and Betty Jeffery publicised their horrific war experiences at home and abroad, after recovering from their wartime ordeal. Both died in the year 2000. Vivian was then aged 84, and Betty Jeffrey (OAM) was 92 when she passed away.

**

WAR INVOLVEMENT FOR
INDIGENOUS AUSTRALIANS

During and before the World War 1 era, Australian aborigines were not even classified as citizens. Under the Commonwealth Protectors' Act, they were not allowed to vote, it was not permissible for them to enter a public bar, they were forbidden to marry a non-indigenous partner, and they were not allowed to purchase property. Indigenous Australians were also banned from enlisting in the armed services.

In actual fact, many aborigines did serve with the military, and they were often better accepted in active combat situations by their digger mates, than they were in civilian life. It is impossible, however, to gain accurate statistics about the number of indigenous Australians who saw active service. Many claimed they were of Maori, Pacific Island or Indian descent in order to be enlisted, so their aboriginality was not revealed to authorities.

However at least 60 Australian aborigines were KIA during World War 1. One of the fallen was Reg Rawlings, the uncle of Reg Saunders, who later became the first aboriginal to receive promotion to a commissioned rank. Reg Rawlings was awarded a Military Medal for the bravery he displayed in the

Great War, and his deeds later inspired his nephew to enlist for military action at the earliest opportunity.

Discriminatory practices still applied to aborigines during the early years of World War 11. Both the Australian Army and Navy excluded "persons not substantially of European descent". The RAAF, largely because of its critical short-age of manpower, was more welcoming to indigenous appli-cants. Once the threat of a Japanese invasion became a real possibility, the Army and Navy services also became more accommodating.

Unofficial figures indicate that at least six aborigines paid the supreme sacrifice in World War 11, while it is recorded that four were KIA in the Vietnam War. Many enlisted in the various wars because there was less discrimination from their serving mates than in mainstream life, and they also received a regular income. Like many young men who enlisted, the conflicts also initially appealed to their sense of adventure. Overall, it appears that at least 3,000 aborigines were actively involved in World War 11 action. Approximately the same number was employed during the conflict as military labourers. Assisting in salvage operations of crashed planes, and locating unexploded bombs, were typical wartime roles designated to aboriginal civilians.

However, aborigines serving in the military, were not awarded valour medals until 1992. Furthermore, soldier set-tlement benefits, which became available for returning Anglo-Saxon Australians in post-war years, did not apply to indigenous ex-servicemen. Many were also scarred by "stolen generation" policies, which resulted in their children being taken from their family homes. Government support for injured or mentally affected indigenous soldiers was very limited. Discriminatory practices of this type, helped advance the Aboriginal Rights Movement, from the 1930s onwards.

Reginald (Reg) Walter Saunders (MBE) remains arguably the most outstanding Australian indigenous soldier. He was a member of the Gunditjmara people, and was born in 1920 near the Framlingham Aboriginal Reserve, on the outskirts of Warrnambool in Victoria. His mother was only a young woman when she died, and Reg's early years were spent at the Lake Condah Mission.

Lieutenant
Reg Saunders

After leaving school at the age of 14, Reg became a mill-hand in a timber yard, but his background indicated that he was born to be a soldier. His father, Chris, and uncle, Reg, both served in World War 1, so Reg Saunders, and later his brother, Harry, enlisted for armed service at the earliest possible age. Unfortunately, Harry Saunders was later KIA, in the New Guinea conflict.

Reg soon proved he was a natural soldier, and he became a popular Non-Commissioned Officer in the 2/7th Battalion. During World War 11, he saw active service in North Africa, and Crete, where friendly locals helped him to avoid enemy capture for several months.

His next military destination was New Guinea, from where he was transferred to an

Officer Training Unit in late 1944. At the conclusion of the course, Reg Saunders became the first aboriginal to be promoted to a commissioned rank, when he was elevated to the status of Lieutenant.

The career soldier then saw action in the Korean War, where he led the C Company 3rd Battalion RAR in April 1951, through fierce engagements at Kapyong. In the Korean conflict, Lieutenant Reg Saunders was nominated for a US Presidential Citation, but the modest, self effacing aboriginal declined the honour.

"There were 25 other blokes in that particular battle with me, and they didn't get any recognition, so why should I?" reasoned Saunders.

Reg Sauders left army service in 1952, and at first he found civilian life in Sydney difficult. A move to Canberra, where he became an officer with the Department of Aboriginal affairs, suited his needs better. This dignified and good humoured man still resided in the national capital, when he died at the age of 69.

Charles Mene, from Mabuiag or Jervis Island in the Torres Strait, was another fine indigenous soldier. After enlisting in the AIF on 15th December 1939, Charles Mene saw action in World War 11. He was a member of occupying forces in Japan and Korea, where he was awarded a Military Medal.

Leonard (Len) Victor Waters was Australia's first indigenous military aviator, and the only aboriginal to serve as an RAAF fighter pilot in World War 11. Len was born in northern NSW, raised in Queensland, and worked as a shearer before joining the RAAF in 1942.

At first he was employed as a mechanic, but he soon volunteered for flying duties, and graduated as a Sergeant Pilot in 1944. By sheer coincidence, the particular P-40 Kittyhawk which he flew was previously named "Black Magic". Len adopted that title with pride, in his 95 completed missions in the Kittyhawk, during the South-West Pacific conflict.

Len Waters

Waters rose to the rank of Warrant Officer. When World War 11 ended, he married Gladys Saunders, with whom he had six children. In civilian life, Len Waters attempted to start a regional airline service, but this dream ended when he was unable to gain adequate financial backing. The setback upset Waters, and he reportedly commented that:

"Once I took off my uniform, I returned to being a black fellow".

The former RAAF pilot also experienced examples of discrimination throughout the war years. During the Pacific conflict, when he was on leave in the NSW town of Moree, Waters was allegedly jailed after failing to produce an identity card. Racial problems such as these usually did not occur when he was on active duty. Waters, who at one stage was the middle weight boxing champion of the RAAF, was remembered by his aviator colleagues, as being a fine pilot, and a genial man.

Len Waters returned to shearing, after his commercial flying ambitions failed to materialise. He was 69 years of age when he died in the Queensland outback town of Cunnamulla.

**

Surprisingly, the Royal Australian Navy, (RAN) has not currently produced an Australian VC winner. One unconvincing explanation about this apparent anomaly, is that it is more difficult to produce substantiated proof about examples of valour in maritime conflicts.

That supposition may soon change. Soon a panel of experts will decide if any or all of 13 newly nominated candidates, will become recipients of this prestigious honour. It is known that at least three of those being considered for VC medals, have previously served with the RAN.

Teddy Sheean

Teddy Sheean: Ordinary Seaman Edward (Teddy) Sheean is a posthumous naval candidate. Teddy was a cheeky, irreverent and likeable teenager (and the youngest in a family of 16) which resided at Lower Barrington in Tasmania. Teddy became a farm labourer, before he volunteered for RAN duties in 1941. The Sheeans have a proud history of enrolling for active service, as five of Teddy's brothers "joined up" in World War 11, before he also became eligible to enlist.

Teddy Sheean was assigned to the corvette

HMAS "Armidale", where he began training as an Oerlikon anti-aircraft gunner. At first "Armidale" was engaged in mundane voyages along Australia's east coast, but soon a more dangerous mission was assigned. "Armidale" began a supply and evacuation exercise to the Japanese controlled island of Timor in the Arafura Sea, which carried the vessel into enemy controlled waters.

In the afternoon of December 1st 1942, Japanese aircraft bombarded the corvette, which began to sink rapidly. An "abandon ship" order was given by the captain, but many of "Armidale's" crew were gunned down once they entered the water.

Ordinary Seaman Sheean did not obey the captain's command. Instead, the wounded youngster strapped himself to his Oerlikon machine gun, and he commenced firing at the Japanese attackers. Sheean shot down at least two enemy planes. Many of the 49 sailors who survived the bombardment, attributed their lives to Teddy Sheean's brave actions.

Even as "Armidale" sank beneath the waves, observers believe tracer bullets were still being fired from the surface of the water, as Ordinary Seaman Sheehan sank to his death. It is estimated that 100 RAN sailors were KIA in that air attack.

Today Teddy Sheean is honoured in a graphic painting depicting his brave actions, and this work is displayed prominently at Canberra's National War Museum. In 1999 a Collins-class submarine was named after Teddy Sheean. This is the first occasion that an Ordinary Seaman has been honoured in this way.

Hec Waller: Captain Hector (Hec) MacDonald Laws Waller

Hec Waller

(DSO and Bar), was 17 years of age, when he became a King's Medal graduate from Australia's RAN College. Waller then saw World War 1 service with the Grand Fleet in Britain for two years, before returning home.

After World War 11 broke out, Hec Waller was given command of HMAS "Stuart", and was assigned for duty in the Mediterranean Sea. German sailors sarcastically called old vessels in this fleet "the scrap iron flotilla", but the RAN ships fulfilled their tasks effectively.

In 1940, Waller was promoted to Captain, which was the first time an Australian was awarded that honour during a time of war. The devoted husband and father of two sons, was given command of the 10th Destroyer Flotilla. During this period of service, Captain Hec Waller was granted a Distinguished Service Order (DSO), and later a Bar was added to this prestigious award. At this time, Waller became involved in many dangerous naval exercises, including the delivery of supplies to the Rats of Tobruk.

In September 1941, Captain Waller took command of the cruiser HMAS "Perth", which was given the testing task of helping defend the Dutch East Indies (now Indonesia), from strong enemy attacks. Observers have since criticised this decision. Significantly, the undermanned fleet was savagely pummelled in the Battle of Java Sea on 27th February 1942, by numerically superior Japanese forces.

Two days later, "Perth" and its sister ship USS "Houston", became engaged in a fierce encounter in the Sunda Strait. Captain Waller resolutely attempted to crash through the large Japanese fleet, but his brave efforts faltered, once "Perth" ran out of ammunition.

"Abandon Ship. Every man for himself," was Captain Waller's last command.

Following this 1941 attack on "Perth", he stayed with his ship, and was KIA after Japanese torpedos sank both his vessel and the "Houston". Hec Waller's calmness in a crisis remained constant, but his decision to remain with his doomed ship, is still regarded as a tragedy. It was a premature end for the 42 year old sailor, who is still considered by many to be the most outstanding naval officer of his generation. In 1997 a Collins-class submarine was named in honour of Hec Waller.

The sinking of "Perth" was a devastating blow to the RAN and the enormity of the loss is echoed by the stanza of verse below, which was penned by an anonymous poet.

**"We lost well nigh four hundred men
From the fairest land on the Earth,
They fought it out to the bitter end
And went down with the Perth."**

Ernest (Ernie) James Noble: Fortunately, Ernie Noble did not go down with the "Perth". However, following his recent death, on 22nd September 2011, only 12 survivors still survive from that famous ship, which sank beneath the waves nearly

70 years ago.

When four Japanese torpedos destroyed the hapless vessel on 1st March 1942, 353 of the 682 sailors on board were killed. Only four of the 329 who survived avoided being captured as POWs. By the time the war ended, 218 of those interned by the Japanese, were still alive. Ernie Noble was one who was miraculously spared. The kindness and efficiency he displayed as a medical orderly, both after "Perth" sank, and later in the hellish POW camps, was never forgotten by his fellow servicemen.

HMAS "Perth"

Ernie Noble was one of seven children, who grew up in the Victorian town of Yarrawonga. By the age of 15 he joined the work force, and for 47 years, (excluding the time spent in war service), Ernie was employed by the Melbourne and Metropolitan Tramways Board.

As a young man, he joined the Navy Reserve, and soon after World War 11 began, Ernie Noble was posted to the ill-fated HMAS "Perth". Only four months later, Ernie was struggling for his life in the waters off Java, after his ship and the USS "Houston" were both sunk by a huge Japanese fleet. It took only ninety minutes for both Allied cruisers to be destroyed, and a massive death toll of 1,090 sailors to be recorded.

The then 23 year old Noble fortunately survived that catastrophic night in centimetre thick fuel oil, which suffocated many of his comrades in the ocean. Around dawn he and 47 other crewmen managed to swim to nearby Sangieng Island. For the next five days Ernie Noble attended to the needs of the injured, and, after reaching Java. most of the survivors decided to attempt to sail to Australia. Noble elected to stay with the wounded, and the small group made the fateful decision to surrender to the Japanese. It soon became obvious that this was a disastrous decision.

They were taken to the Javanese town of Serang, which Ernie later described as **"…a terrible, terrible place. I don't know how we survived the next few weeks; it was unbelievable…"**

Noble's cell was built to hold seven prisoners, but at least 25 men were crammed into the small confine. Dirty brown rice and water was their only food, which was made available twice a day.

The POWs were then sent to the notorious Burma-Thailand railway project, to help build a 415 kilometre supply link through the jungle terrain. Starvation, cholera, dysentery and malaria were rife in the camps, and Noble tended to hundreds of men who were dying before his eyes.

Somehow Ernie survived the horrors of "death railroad". He returned to Melbourne, where he and wife Mavis raised a family of three daughters. He resumed work with the tramways until his retirement. He also became secretary of the HMAS Perth Association when it was first founded, and provided 60 years of dedicated service to this organisation.

When Ernie Noble died recently in Epworth Hospital Richmond, after enduring a long period of illness, a naval mate provided the following heartfelt tribute:

"He was the stuff of heroes".

Fred Lasslett: Melbourne born Fred Lasslett was an Electrical Wireman assigned to "Perth". After he jumped off the sinking ship, Fred clung to floatable objects in the oily water for at least ten hours, before he and other Australian survivors, were picked up by a Japanese boat. He then spent three years as a Japanese POW in Java, Singapore and Japan.

Thankfully Fred Lasslett survived his long imprisonment. On returning to civilian life in Melbourne, he married, raised four children, and in 2009 wrote "War Diaries", a book which provides fascinating insights about his wartime experiences.

Richard Emms: Francis Bassett "Richard" Emms is the third RAN contender to come under consideration for a VC medal. Emms suffered stomach wounds aboard HMAS "Kara Kara" while Darwin was being bombed in 1942. He stoically ignored his injuries, and mounted a brave machine gun attack against the enemy.

"Weary" Dunlop: In the life threatening environment of World War 11 Japanese prison camps, some brave Australians became inspirational figures. The most well known and most loved such person, was probably Ernest Edward "Weary" Dunlop.

"Weary" Dunlop

Dunlop was born in 1907, and in his youth he was a champion athlete, who gained selection as a Wallaby in the Australian Rugby Union team. He was also an exceptional scholar, who became a doctor, and later a Fellow of London's Royal College of Surgeons. Dunlop also became a Captain in the Australian Medical Corps, (AMC).

After volunteering for World War 11 action in Greece and North Africa, his troopship was diverted to Java. There Lieutenant-Colonel Dunlop was captured by the Japanese at Bandung in 1942, and he became a POW at Changi in Singapore.

By January 1943, Dunlop became the commander of the first Australian POWs assigned to work on what became notoriously remembered as the Burma-Thailand railway. The evil project was soon dubbed "death railroad", which reportedly cost a life for every 25 metres of track which was laid. At least 16,000 POWs perished in the jungle terrain, during the 16 months of construction.

The Burma-Thai railway was also a disaster for those who somehow survived. Food was totally inadequate, beatings from their cruel captors were both frequent and brutal, and severe tropical diseases became rampant, due to the lack of essential medicines.

In this unbelievably harsh environment, "Weary" Dunlop became what one inmate described as **"A lighthouse of sanity in a universe of madness and suffering"**.

Dunlop's dedication and selflessness became legendary among his fellow prisoners, and his medical skills and compassion encouraged high group morale in the horrific prison camps, and grossly inadequate hospital tents.

"In suffering we are all equal," was the mantra Dunlop followed.

Once peace was declared in 1945, "Weary", (his nickname somehow originated from Dunlop tyres), generously forgave his Japanese captors. He devoted himself to the welfare of former POWs and their families, and he attempted to foster better relations with Asian countries. Dunlop also returned to the medical profession, and his work in cancer research gained him many honours throughout the world.

The much loved and talented Lieutenant-Colonel Sir Ernest Edward "Weary" Dunlop passed away in Melbourne in 1993. He was then 86 years of age, and today a memorial statue in the Benalla Botanical Gardens honours the man and his achievements.

**

OTHER CHANGI HEROES

POWs had no weapons to defend themselves from their often

cruel captors. Instead they relied on their mateship, a usually optimistic outlook, and their sense of humour, to survive the endless drudgery and hardship of life in a POW camp.

Sport was a wonderful diversion. Ben Barnett, a classy wicketkeeper who represented Australia in four cricket Tests, was an inmate at Changi. He organised Ashes matches between the "Brits" and the "Aussies" within the camp grounds, and these "Tests" were popular with both players and spectators.

Wilfred "Chicken" Smallhorn,

Wilfred "Chicken" Smallhorn, formerly a brilliant wingman with VFL club Fitzroy, and the 1933 Brownlow Medallist, helped organise a six-team VFL type competition. The Changi league had around 200 registered players, two appointed umpires, and a tribunal which handed down fines or suspensions, for any serious misdemeanours by players.

Movement of players between teams was allowed, and three bowls of rice was considered a reasonable transfer fee for a footballer from a rival team. Their football ground was carved out of thick jungle, and the best and fairest player was awarded the highly esteemed Changi Brownlow. The medal was reportedly made of metal from a downed Japanese aeroplane. The proud 1942 winner was Corporal Leslie Allan "Peter" Chitty, who previously played two VFL games with St. Kilda.

Corporal Leslie
Allan "Peter" Chitty

Peter Chitty originated from a large rural family near Cudgewa, in the ruggedly beautiful Upper Murray area of Victoria. He was one of seven siblings who volunteered for World War 11 service. A brother was KIA at El Alamein in North Africa, while two other siblings became POW's in Crete. Another brother, Bob Chitty, moved to Melbourne, where he became a champion footballer with VFL club, Carlton.

Back home, Peter Chitty had worked as a farm hand. This typical Aussie country bloke became an inspiration in Changi, on the sporting arena, in the war zones, and on the infamous Burma-Thai Railway.

After enlisting, Peter Chitty devoted himself to saving lives, when he became an ambulance driver with the Australian 8th Division in Singapore. When the Japanese military began heavily bombing the city area, Chitty often risked his life in rescue operations.

The unassuming Australian had a keen sense of humour. On one occasion, a Japanese guard intercepted Chitty when he was smuggling food into the camp.

"What's this?" asked the suspicious soldier on sentry duty, as he waved a jar of vegemite in the Aussie's face.

"Boot polish, mate," replied Peter promptly.

The disbelieving guard motioned Chitty to remove the vegemite lid. The Australian obliged, smeared some of the black substance on his own boot, and began polishing motions with his hand.

The sentry was convinced, and waved Peter on.

On another occasion, Peter was one of many POWs who were ordered to assemble, with their tin mugs, to honour the Japanese Emperor's birthday. For the celebratory occasion, an officer provided a small measure of saki for the prisoners, so they could toast their enemy's leader.

The situation grew tense when the POWs at first failed to comply. Then Vern Rae, a POW who was formerly an Intelligence Officer with the Australian 15th battery, stepped forward.

"Boys, we drink to the Emperor. Faaark the Emperor," he shouted defiantly, before draining the contents of his mug.

The other prisoners followed his example, but their host was keen to display his understanding of the English/ Australian language.

" Faaark the Emperor," yelled the Japanese officer, with great gusto. Many encores were then rendered, both by him, and the laughing Aussies.

Peter Chitty became a legend during the four harrowing years he endured on the Burma-Thai railway. Like all the other underfed POWs, Chitty became dangerously emaciated. He only weighed 78 kilograms when he heroically carried a malaria infected cobber, as well as two packs on his back, for over 150 kilometres along the track.

The weight Peter Chitty carried on that arduous journey was more than his own body weight. Little wonder that he suffered severe back problems for the remainder of his life.

Chitty's actions were typical of the spirit of mateship which permeated the POW camps along the railway. In one large camp a serious outbreak of cholera killed over 30 prisoners in just one day. Bruce Hunt, a medical doctor with the group, warned the other POWs they could easily become infected themselves, before he asked for volunteers to care for cholera sufferers. Reportedly, 120 men immediately put their own lives on the line, and offered their services.

When the surviving POWs were liberated at the end of the war, Peter Chitty was awarded a British Empire Medal. Only 24 such medals were awarded to World War 11 prisoners, but the self effacing Chitty appeared more impressed by his 1942 Changi Brownlow award. In typical fashion, included his mates in the Empire medal honour.

"We all gave 100% of what we could," stated Chitty.

Peter Chitty was survived by his widow Lillian and four children, when he passed away at the age of 84.

Tony Gaze: The Melbourne-born Frederick Anthony Owen (Tony) Gaze was destined to lead an adventurous life. His father, Irvine Gaze, was a member of the Ross Sea party in Ernest Shackleton's expedition to Antarctica, and Tony Gaze was raised in a privileged and well educated family. The Gaze's established the financially successful Ezy Walking Shoe Company, and when World War 11 began, Tony Gaze was a student at the prestigious Oxford University in England.

After volunteering for active service, Tony Gaze's achievements as a RAF fighter pilot in wartime Europe became impressive. Gaze was the first Australian to become a squadron leader of an allied jet air wing, when he assumed command of the RAF 616 Squadron. He was also the first allied pilot to land in France after D–Day, and the first Australian to shoot down a ME 612 jet in a combat situation. In the closing stages of the war, Tony Gaze also became the first Australian jet fighter pilot.

During combat over Europe, Gaze not only survived an aircraft crash in occupied France; he also greatly assisted local French resistance forces, before returning safely to England. By the war's end, Tony Gaze was a highly regarded airman, and he became the only World War 11 Australian to receive a Distinguished Flying Cross (DFC) with two Bars.

Tony Gaze

During Gaze's 488 war missions, his strike rate of victories was an impressive 12.5. This statistic placed Tony Gaze in tenth position, alongside wartime aviation luminaries such as Wing Commander Douglas "tin legs" Bader, spitfire war ace Johnnie Johnson, and Paul Tibbets, the pilot who dropped an atomic bomb over Hiroshima.

Back in mainstream life, Tony Gaze continued his adventurous pursuits. After competing in the 1952 Belgian Grand Prix, Gaze became Australia's first official racing car driver. In this role, he competed internationally in open wheel and sports car racing events. Eight years later, Gaze represented Australia in the World Gliding Championships in Germany.

After car racing legend Lex Davidson lost his life at the wheel, Tony Gaze later married Davidson's widow, Diana. He continued his own racing career, and in 2006 he received an Order of Australia (OAM) for his services to the motor racing industry.

In more recent years author Stewart Wilson wrote Tony Gaze's biography, which is titled "Almost Unknown".

Jack Sue

Jack Sue: The son of an illegal immigrant father from China, and an Australian born mother, Jack experienced racism, in various forms, throughout much of his life. During World War 11, Sue became both a highly accomplished RAAF officer, and a brilliant behind-enemy-lines operator.

Jack Sue was seconded to the Z Special Unit, (an allied intelligence and commando unit), from the RAAF. In his undercover role he proved to be invaluable with the contributions he gleaned from enemy territory in South-East Asia. In his espionage role Jack Sue's Asian appearance, and his ability to speak fluent Malay and Chinese, proved to be crucial. He worked behind enemy lines for months at a time. During his long tours of duty it was estimated that he and other Z commandos killed 1,700 Japanese soldiers, and trained 6,000 indigenous recruits in warfare techniques.

Jack also became familiar with harrowing experiences. While working undercover in Borneo, he discovered "the POW camp from hell", where less than ten of an original 2,000 Australian prisoners survived their captivity under the Japanese invaders.

In 1950 Jack Sue was awarded a Distinguished Conduct Medal, (DCM), for displaying "leadership, gallantry and cold blooded courage of the highest order". After returning to civilian life in Western Australia, Jack Sue operated a diving school. He also became the author of a book titled "Blood in Bornco", and the co-author of "Ghost of the Alkimos".

After this war hero died in 2009 at the age of 84, State Premier, Colin Barnett, described Jack Sue as **"A true hero during some of the darkest days in Australian history".**

George Buckworth was only 17 years of age, when he falsified his birth date, and volunteered for service with the RAAF. A year later the son of a Boer War veteran became a commissioned officer, and a navigator with the Bomber Command 75 Squadron. During the course of World War 11, George Buckworth also became the youngest Squadron Leader in the RAAF.

George Buckworth

Buckworth evaded enemy captors for days, after being shot down over Belgium in 1942. He was later awarded the Croix de Guerre, for not disclosing vital information about local resistance forces, after he was finally captured and interrogated.

As a POW, Buckworth's continual optimism and support for fellow in-mates, was much admired, during the 22 months he was held prisoner. When World War 11 ended, the irrepressible adventurer led a squadron of Dakota DC3s in an epic flight from Canada to Sydney. Buckworth celebrated his 21st birthday, on the day he touched down in Australia.

Before long George Buckworth was recruited by ASIO. In that covert role he safeguarded Evdokia Petrov, when aggressive Russian KGB agents attempted to forcibly remove her from Darwin airport, in April 1954.

George and his wife, whom he first met when they were both students at Sydney Law School, settled for some years in Broken Hill, where the war hero became a local legend, after setting up a joint legal practice in the large mining town.

George Buckworth revealed impressive entrepreneurial skills. He built the largest drive-in theatre in the southern hemisphere, and he also operated a bakery, finance company, laundry, three hotels, and a ski chalet at Mt. Kosciusko.

In later years George established a legal practice back in Sydney, before he prematurely retired to care for his now invalided wife. The ebullient 85 year old was survived by his wife, three children, eight grandchildren and three great grandchildren, when he passed away in 2009.

"Killer" Caldwell: Clive Robertson "Killer" Caldwell was born in Sydney, and educated at Sydney Grammar School. When World War 11 began, Caldwell was too old to volunteer for service, but he modified his birth certificate, and enlisted in the RAAF.

In 1941 Clive Caldwell graduated as a Pilot Officer from the Empire Air Training Scheme, and went on to fly 250 missions over Syria, Palestine and North Africa.

"Killer" Caldwell

His first war victory was recorded on 26th June, 1941. Overall, his impressive combat air strike rate of 20.5 earned him the nickname of "Killer", which was a title he disliked.

During January 1942, "Killer Caldwell was given command of the 112 Squadron RAAF, and in that role he was awarded both the Polish Cross of Valour as well as a DFC and Bar.

After being transferred home to help defend Darwin, Caldwell added eight Japanese aircraft to his impressive tally of victories, before taking on the role of Chief Flying Instructor.

Caldwell regarded this stint with the RAAF as being both pointless and boring, and he was a bitter and disillusioned man when he resigned his post in 1946.

"Killer" Caldwell, who recorded the highest total of "hits" by an Australian in World War 11, was aged 84 when he passed away in Sydney in 1994.

CHAPTER NINETEEN

HEROES ALL: THE DECORATED, THE LITTLE KNOWN, AND THE UNKNOWING

"Cowards die many times before their death;
The valiant never taste of death but once."
(Quote from William Shakespeare's 'Julius Caesar').

It is fascinating to muse about what motivates our VC winners, (and countless other unnamed courageous service personnel, who perform many reckless deeds of bravery.

In some instances, their courageous actions appear to accurately reflect their everyday personalities. If Wally Brown was still miraculously alive, after defiantly walking towards armed Japanese soldiers with grenades in hand, he would probably have enjoyed parachuting or bungy-jumping.

The same hypothetical suppositions could apply to many other extroverted characters, such as Fred Bell, Maurice

Buckley, John Carroll, Percy Cherry, Joergen Jensen, Laurie McCarthy, Rupert Moon, John Whittle and "Dasher" Wheatley. Their demeanour in battle, and the life styles they chose, suggests they were probably dare-devils in everyday life. However, others appeared to adopt completely different personas, once they became involved in dangerous combat situations.

Lone Pine hero Bill Dunstan was a reserved person, who shunned any public acclaim about his war-time achievements. Outwardly, Albert Borella showed little of the steely determination, which characterised his behaviour on the Western Front. Bill Jackson was a shy and reticent man. Wally Peeler and Cliff Sadlier also appeared to have been modest and private men in civilian life. Frank McNamara, the larger than life hero of the dramatic desert rescue at Tel el Hesi, was usually a gentle and scholarly man.

Sir Arthur Roden Cutler, a charming and sophisticated World War 11 veteran, became highly valued for his international diplomatic skills. Peter Badcoe was conservative in nature, and a devoted husband and family man away from the battlefields of Vietnam. In these and other examples, the war action "adrenalin rush", which precipitated their particular acts of bravery, produced reactions which appeared to be totally out of character.

The soldiers referred to in the above two paragraphs, have all been deservedly decorated for their acts of valour. However, there are countless other heroes, whose brave deeds are not widely known or acclaimed

In her engrossing book, "Unsung Ordinary Men", Sally Dingo eulogises some relatives from her own family, as well as other war veterans who resided in her Tasmanian home town

of Penguin. The heroes Sally describes were obviously courageous people, but their deeds and post-war problems remain
largely unknown to the general public. She aptly sums up
their mostly anonymous wartime achievements, in the para-
graph quoted below.

**"...(it is) a story of courage and sacrifice and endurance
beyond belief, of these ordinary Australian men from
ordinary backgrounds - farm labourers, cabinet makers,
concrete workers...**

**I have come to believe, that for many of these unsung
ordinary men, who were not heroes, the word 'hero' will
never be enough".**

What characteristics then, do all heroes have in common?
Vietnam veteran John "Jethro" Thomson, (a hero to all, excluding himself), has some interesting views on the subject.

From Thomson's experience of life, heroes do not come
from any specific group or personality type. Those who we see
decorated for their brave acts on television news can be young,
old, big, small, male, female, and slim or overweight. The circumstances which produced their acts of bravery are of paramount importance, as true heroism cannot be fabricated.

Furthermore, among people in our very own environment,
some unknowing heroes may reside. Few of us know, with
any certainty, how we will react if a single brave act is needed
to overcome a particular crisis. Furthermore, heroic deeds performed in one dangerous scenario do not automatically transfer
to another. Consequently, individuals suddenly thrust into
a perilous environment, are often totally unaware that they

possess heroic traits, until they are forced to react to a particular set of circumstances. It is only after their often spontaneous actions resolve or improve a crisis situation, that the label of "hero" can be accurately assigned.

The few decorated heroes Jethro Thomson knows are ordinary people, who simply did what they were expected to do. Fortunately, their courage and skill was observed by others, which resulted in well deserved recognition for their heroic deeds. In summary, Jethro Thomson believes that,

"Heroism is a combination of an individual's desire to assist people in danger, even though they risk death or injury themselves."

On Thompson's overall analysis, the personalities and lifestyles of heroes are widely diverse. The one common factor, especially in wartime situations, often appears to be the factor of mateship.

Mateship is often associated with Australians from all walks of life, but it is not unique to our culture. In fact, as Monash University Australian Studies lecturer, Nick Dryenfurth, revealed in an article on "The Age" on Australia Day 2012, the term "mate" is derived from the old German word "gemate", a word which means "sharing one's meat with a friend".

Nevertheless, for at least the past two centuries, Australian men and women of all political persuasions, have either lauded or castigated the traditions of Australian mateship. In fact, for a nation that is now often dismissive about spiritual beliefs, mateship has at times appeared to be a de facto religion, and an essential part of our national identity.

In his fascinating book, titled "The Australian Legend", Russel Ward advances the view that that the bonds of mateship were first forged from the anti-authoritarian attitudes of convict society. By the mid 1880s mateship grew even stronger among seasonal workers in remote areas. It is still seen as being a characteristic of rough and ready "dinkum" Aussies, who despise both authoritarianism and any appearance of affectation in others.

Mateship is still sometimes associated exclusively with the heroic deeds of Australian soldiers, but its origins began earlier in our history. In 1893 William "Billy" Lane, and 220 of his followers, sailed from our shores, to the remote South American country of Paraguay, where they set up a "utopian" settlement known as "New Australia". There the group was governed by strict laws of temperance and racial exclusiveness, and it was anticipated that "mateship" would bond them closely together in this "socialist Eden." Ironically, when the experiment failed, "Billy Lane" became a noted conservative imperialist, after his family and he relocated to New Zealand.

Mateship is still a concept, however, which is embraced by both modern conservative and Labor politicians. In 1999, Liberal Prime John Howard insisted that mateship was a "hallowed Australian word", and on Australia Day 2011, the incumbent Labor Prime Minister, Julia Gillard, asserted that "mateship defines our nation".

Endurance, courage and a willingness to sacrifice everything for your partner, family member, friend, comrade in arms, or even a stranger, can all collectively fall under the umbrella of mateship. A soldier especially knows he can trust his mates to save him, in life threatening situations.

In the dead of night on 25th June 1916, near Armentieres in France, one badly wounded Aussie World War 1 digger, luckily found the truest of all army mates in Private Bill Jackson. Bill ignored severe pain from his badly wounded shoulder, when he carried his injured mate through heavy fire to safety. By then Jackson's arm was nearly severed from his shoulder, and it later had to be amputated.

This brave act of loyalty, from a shy and reticent man, was accurately placed in context in July 1917, at a public welcome in the NSW town of Hay. At the reception in honour of Sergeant Cambden and Private Jackson, Cambden spoke emotionally about the new VC's brave rescue, and informed the gathering that **"Bill was not looking for a VC that night. He was looking for a cobber."**

Similar bonds of mateship motivated a quiet man like Wally Peeler to charge fearlessly towards heavily armed enemy trenches in World War 1. During the same war, it was mateship which persuaded Percy Statton to rescue his commander from a perilous situation.

Sometimes a form of mateship even appears to transfer across enemy lines. At Gallipoli in World War 1, and Tobruk in World War 11, ceasefires were mutually agreed to, so soldiers from both sides could take a meal break or attend to burying their dead. In these treasured moments of peace, cigarettes, food and conversation were sometimes exchanged between rival soldiers, before armed hostilities were resumed from their respective trenches.

...I am the enemy you killed, my friend
I knew you in this dark;
For so you frowned yesterday through me
As you jabbed and killed...

This stanza of verse is quoted from Wilfred Owen's acclaimed poem, "Strange Meeting". Owen was a World War 1 enigma; a soldier who became a tormented pacifist, after experiencing the horrors of the Western Front, but who still gained a posthumous Military Cross (MC), for his fearless acts of bravery at Joncourt. Sadly Wilfred Owen was KIA in that battle, and his death occurred only a week before peace was declared.

In the above extract from "Strange Meeting", Owen imagines a sad but respectful after-life meeting with a German soldier he had killed. It mirrors an actual encounter, which the late Captain Percy Cherry experienced on the Western Front.

It was at Lagnicourt in France in March 1917, that Cherry displayed a similar feeling of respectful mateship to an enemy soldier. Both he and his German opponent were badly wounded during a one-off gun battle, but the dying German managed to pass on some of his personal letters to his assailant. Percy Cherry needed to recuperate for months after surviving the gun battle, but he still honoured his word to the enemy soldier he had slain, and posted off the correspondence when he was recovering from his war wounds.

In wartime action, soldiers share their mates' tragedies and triumphs. Consequently, in August 1917, fellow diggers in the 33rd Battalion cheered George Cartwright to the echo, after he captured nine Germans and a machine gun, near Peronne on the Western Front.

The same renowned spirit of comradeship prevailed on the Kokoda Trail during World War 11, when an inspired Bruce Kingsbury fearlessly "took on" an advancing group of Japanese with his Bren gun. Kingsbury's brave action helped the besieged Aussies cling to their fortified position at Isurava, until welcome reinforcements arrived.

In Vietnam, mateship compelled "Dasher" Wheatley to sacrifice his own life, rather than leave a badly wounded comrade to be captured by enemy forces. Mark Donaldson was also a true mate to the wounded colleague he carried to safety, during a fierce 2008 Taliban attack in Afghanistan.

Shakespeare may be correct when he asserts that "the valiant never taste of death but once". However, in a wartime environment, when the characters and personalities of soldiers differ greatly, perhaps mateship becomes the strongest motivating factor, when brave actions become necessary in life-threatening situations.

It is difficult to disagree with Sally Dingo's assertion that the word "hero" will never be enough, to describe the brave past and present service men and women, who defend their family, friends and country from the threat of enemy aggression.

BIBLIOGRAPHY

ABC DVDs "Australians at War", (Episodes 1-4 & 5-8).

Adam-Smith, Patsy, "Prisoners of War", Viking Penguin Books Australia (1992).

The Age (April 2011- March 2012).

Australian War Museum research visit (April, 2011).

Battle, Captain M.R. (editor) "The Year of the Tigers", 5th Battalion Royal Australian Regiment (1970).

Canberra Times newspaper (April, 2011).

Carlyon, Les, "Gallipoli", Pan Macmillan Australia Pty, Ltd (2001).

Clark, Manning, "A Short History of Australia", Mentor Books USA (1963).

Dingo, Sally, "Unsung Ordinary Men", Hachette Australia (2010).

Ferguson, Ian, "Disasters that Shocked Australia", Brolga Publishing Pty Ltd Company (2009).

Fitzsimons, Peter, "Kokoda", Hachette Australia (2004).

Hamilton, John, "Goodbye Cobber, God Bless You", Pan Macmillan Australia Pty Ltd (2004).

Lasslett, Fred, "War Diaries, Japanese POW", Brolga Publishing Company (2006).

Lawriwsky, Michael "Return of the Gallipoli Legend, Albert Jacka", Mira Books, Chatswood, NSW (2010).

Perry, Roland, "The Australian Light Horse", Hachette Australia (2009).

Perry, Roland, "The Changi Brownlow", Hachette Australia (2010).

Ward, Russel, "The Australian Legend", Oxford University Press, Melbourne (1958).

Wikipedia - the Free Encyclopaedia www.wikipedia.com (2011).

INDEX

THEY SHALL NOT GROW OLD

AUSTRALIAN WAR HEROES

Ian Ferguson

ISBN 9781922036520			Qty
	RRP	AU$26.99	.....
Postage within Australia		AU$5.00	.....
		TOTAL* $_____	
		* All prices include GST	

Name: ....

Address: ....

....

Phone: ....

Email: ....

Payment: ❑ Money Order ❑ Cheque ❑ Amex ❑ MasterCard ❑ Visa

Cardholders Name: ....

Credit Card Number: ....

Signature: ....

Expiry Date: ....

Allow 21 days for delivery.

Payment to: Marzocco Consultancy (ABN 14 067 257 390)
                  PO Box 12544
                  A'Beckett Street, Melbourne, 8006
                  Victoria, Australia
                  Fax: +61 3 9671 4730
                  admin@brolgapublishing.com.au

Publishing through a successful Australian publisher. Brolga provides:
- Editorial appraisal
- Cover design
- Typesetting
- Printing
- Author promotion
- National book trade distribution, including sales, marketing and distribution through Macmillan Australia.
- International book trade distribution
- World-wide e-Book distribution

For details and inquiries, contact:
Brolga Publishing Pty Ltd
PO Box 12544
A'Beckett St VIC 8006

Phone: 0414 608 494
admin@brolgapublishing.com.au
markzocchi@brolgapublishing.com.au
ABN: 46 063 962 443